Unbelievable Crimes Volume Ten

Unbelievable Crimes, Volume 10

Daniela Airlie

Published by Daniela Airlie, 2024.

While every precaution has been taken in the preparation of this book, the publisher assumes no responsibility for errors or omissions, or for damages resulting from the use of the information contained herein.

UNBELIEVABLE CRIMES VOLUME TEN

First edition. March 29, 2024.

Copyright © 2024 Daniela Airlie.

Written by Daniela Airlie.

Table of Contents

Unbelievable Crimes Volume Ten 1

Introduction 3

Lady Sundown 5

A Woodland Nightmare 23

Deranged Dad 33

Serve and Protect 43

The "Friendly" Neighborhood Monster 55

A Mile From Home 71

Multiple Missed Opportunities 81

The Beauty Queen Killer 91

The Bus Ride From Hell 103

Final Thoughts 109

The right of Daniela Airlie as the publisher and owner of this work has been asserted in accordance with the Copyright, Designs, and Patents Act 1988. No part of this publication may be reproduced in any format without the publisher's prior written consent. This book is for entertainment and informational purposes only.

Although research from various sources has gone into this book, neither the author nor publisher will be held responsible for any inaccuracies. To the best of the author's knowledge, all information within this publication is factually correct and derived from researching these cases thoroughly. The author may offer speculation and/or opinion about the cases covered throughout this book.

Danielaairlie.carrd.co[1]

---

1. http://danielaairlie.carrd.co

Introduction

Welcome to the tenth installment of *Unbelievable Crimes*.

In this anthology, I'll cover more twisted tales of the macabre, most of which have either been tucked away in the archives of true crime or simply never received much press coverage.

In *Volume Ten*, I delve into a tale of a wicked teenager who, along with her older husband, captured and abused young victims for their sick pleasure. Then there's the case of a father who abused his daughter's trust and loyalty, torturing her before her untimely and terrifying death.

I also cover a more high-profile case from the UK, the murder of Sarah Everard. While it was mainstream news in Britain, it's lesser known around the world, despite the impact it had on the UK and the trust their people had in the police force.

Then there's the tragic case of a young girl who was making her way home from a friend's house, only to be intercepted by a depraved monster.

These crimes, plus seven more true tales, make up the tenth installment of this series. As always, I'd like to offer a word of caution about some of the cases in this book. These crimes are especially brutal to learn about, some of which involve sexual assault, torture, or crimes involving vulnerable individuals.

With that said, if you're ready, let's begin.

Lady Sundown

Wicked women are a fascinating category of true crime stories. Women are nowhere near as murderous as men, but when they *do* have that lust for blood, they're sometimes more sadistic than their male counterparts.

What's more disturbing than a wicked woman? A wicked girl, perhaps. And that's just what Judith Neelley was.

Born Judith Ann Adams in Murfreesboro, Tennessee, in June 1964, not a great deal is known about her early childhood and upbringing. It's reported that her father, who died when she was nine, was an alcoholic. There are no real details about Judith's early teenage years, either, other than suggestions that her mother regularly brought different men home to their trailer.

When she was 15, Judith met Alvin Neelley, a 26-year-old married man. Despite the 11-year age gap and the fact that Judith was a child, Alvin took it upon himself to pursue a relationship with her. By the time Judith had turned 16, Alvin had divorced his wife and eloped with his young bride.

Alvin was a petty criminal, robbing stores and gas stations to make ends meet. A job simply didn't fit into the transient lifestyle he adopted for himself and his teenage spouse. The man would teach Judith his corrupt ways, involving her heavily in his increasingly violent crimes.

In 1980, they headed to Riverbend Mall in Georgia to carry out an armed robbery. Instead, they ended up robbing a woman, holding her at gunpoint as they looted the terrified victim's bag and pockets.

It didn't take long for the police to catch up with the criminals after they tried to cash some of the stolen checks. Alvin was already wanted for a rap sheet of other crimes, but this would be Judith's first run-in with the law.

Alvin got five years in jail, while 16-year-old Judith - who was pregnant at this point - was sent to a youth development center. She was seen, perhaps correctly at this time, as being corrupted by her older husband. The teenager gave birth to twins while she was detained.

However, her run-in with the law didn't quell Judith's love and yearning for her husband. She wrote him dozens of letters while she was at the youth facility and told Alvin that she was being mistreated and sexually abused by the center staff. These claims have never been proven nor disproven, though Alvin naturally believed them to be true. So, he would sit in his prison cell and seethe over the alleged injustices and assaults his wife was enduring. He swore he'd get revenge.

Judith, too, wanted revenge.

She was released earlier than her husband, in late 1981. She couldn't move back with her mother, and with two young children to take care of, she needed help. So, she moved in with Alvin's mother and father. By this point, Judith had learned how to acquire money quickly, and it wasn't by working. Soon after moving back to Tennessee to live with Alvin's parents, she was holding up convenience stores. Without her husband there to guide her, she quickly found herself making mistakes and was re-arrested.

It wasn't long before Judith was free again, though. After all, she wasn't seen as anything more than a wayward teen who couldn't do much, if any, harm. How wrong that perception was.

Six months later, Alvin was released after serving less than half his sentence. Just like his young wife, his stint in jail had taught him nothing. He had no remorse, repentance, or desire to live a crime-free life. In fact, upon leaving prison, he was filled with rage and anger toward the youth development center, who had allegedly wronged his wife. Revenge consumed him.

They picked up their children from his parent's house and set out on the road again. Together, they plotted and schemed how they'd exact their revenge on the development center staff. They batted around ideas, but while they were making their vengeful plans, they figured they needed money to get by. Again, the couple resorted to crime. They would stealthily make their way into post offices and steal checks, using the signatures to produce fake money orders, which they'd cash.

To avoid detection or suspicion, the couple worked alone. They were all too aware of their criminal status as a couple and wanted to avoid recognition. However, Alvin installed a CB radio in each of their cars, and the thieving couple kept in touch with each other that way. It was the early '80s, after all, and mobile phones were years away from being accessible to the general public. So, they made their own means of communication and even gave themselves their own CB handles.

Alvin called himself "Nightrider." Judith named herself "Lady Sundown."

They'd bounce from hotel to motel. While the criminal couple were on their illicit road trip, they encountered a woman they both took a shine to. The pair invited her back to their hotel room, an invite she accepted. Perhaps it was intuition or the fact that she only accepted the invite out of politeness, but the woman never turned up at the agreed time. She didn't know it then, but she very likely saved herself a world of suffering and maybe even avoided her own death by bailing on the date.

It's clear that Alvin and Judith were talking about their fantasies and were looking at ways to make them a reality. Only, their fantasies weren't harmless fun. They were horrifically violent, nightmarish desires.

In the autumn of 1982, the couple decided it was finally time to take their revenge on two employees from the youth detention center. First was Kenneth Dooley, who reported gunshots toward his home on the night of September 11. Then, Linda Adair had a Molotov cocktail hurled onto her driveway the following evening.

Nobody was injured in the attacks. The victims were shaken up, though, and neither of them had any idea who did this or why anyone would target them. A sinister clue made its way to Linda while the police were investigating the crime. She received a phone call from an angry woman who claimed both Linda and her coworker Kenneth would be dead before sunrise.

Later that day, another menacing call from the same woman was recorded at the Floyd County Sheriff's Office. "For the abuse I took, they're both going to die," the caller spat. Still, the caller was unknown, and the number was untraceable. Perhaps a bored juvenile or a wayward teenager getting some twisted kicks, the police thought.

A fortnight later, the criminal couple would embark on some truly despicable crimes.

Teenager Lisa Ann Millican resided at Ethel Harpst, a home for neglected and abused youths. The home was located in Cedartown, Georgia, and offered the 13-year-old girl stability and routine. It also afforded her a small friendship group, with whom she attended the Riverbend Mall on September 25, 1982.

Lisa ended up getting separated from her friends and had the utter misfortune of happening upon Alvin and Judith Neelley. The couple lured the teen to a nearby arcade under the ruse of playing games. Lisa was excited at the prospect of playing the latest arcade games for free, but instead, wound up in a motel in Alabama, bound and stripped of her clothes.

The terrified teen, while cuffed to the bed, noticed two small children roaming about the dank room she was unwillingly in. The Neelley's toddler twins were about to bear witness to every bit of the suffering the teenager endured at the hands of her captors.

This was just the beginning of Lisa's three-day ordeal. The hellish 72 hours were filled with sexual assaults, and not just at the hands of Alvin. Judith also abused Lisa. The sadistic couple would torture their captive and, when they slept, forced the teen onto the floor to sleep, although I can't imagine Lisa did much sleeping, considering the unimaginable situation she was in. She was bound by the wrists to the frame of the bed, unable to free herself no matter how much strength she tried to muster up.

Lisa was no physical match for her attackers, not for Alvin in particular. He was heavyset, sadistic, and determined to ensure the victim wouldn't get out alive. Judith was tall and slender, though her violent streak and lack of empathy made her just as formidable as her husband.

After three days of torturing the teen, Alvin and Judith agreed they'd take Lisa to a desolate canyon to kill her.

What happened next varies slightly depending on whose version of events you want to believe. What we do know for certain is that, once at the canyon, Lisa was injected with drain cleaner by Judith in order to kill her. One syringe into her neck did nothing but cause the teenager unimaginable pain. Judith - who, by Alvin's account, was on her own - stood by and watched as Lisa didn't succumb to the injection. Judith had wrongly assumed one injection of the fluid would be enough to end her life, albeit in a drawn-out manner.

So, Judith inflicted another syringe full of drain cleaner into the teenager's neck. Searing, burning agony filled the girl's veins, but death didn't spare her from any more suffering. She was very much alive after not just two but six syringes filled with drain cleaner were injected into her body. She was alive - but in excruciating pain.

By this point, half an hour after the first injection, it became apparent to Judith that she was going to have to rethink her means of killing Lisa. All the while she was injecting the girl, she had a .38 pistol in her possession. If she only wanted to kill the victim, it seems that a gun would be the quickest and easiest way to do it. The fact that she chose to inject Lisa with drain cleaner instead shows that pain and terror were aspects of the murder she included on purpose.

The definition of a torture murder is one that is inflicted with "exceptional brutality or cruelty."

Pulling out the gun she'd had on her person all along, Judith ordered the victim to the edge of the canyon and shot her in the back. Judith hoped the gunshots would cause Lisa to fall off the edge and tumble down the canyon to certain death. Instead, the shot caused the teenager to fall backward.

Judith walked over to the lifeless body and flung it over the cliff edge. She stood atop the canyon and watched the 13-year-old's limp body hurtle to the ground.

We know all of this to be true. However, Judith and Alvin have conflicting stories about whether he was actually present at the murder or not. Judith says he was, and not only that, but he performed an indecent act on himself after watching the teen thrown over the cliff. Alvin claimed it was all Judith, and he was with his toddlers while she was killing Lisa.

Judith got blood spatters on her jeans from the shooting, prompting her to take them off and toss them down into the canyon with the body.

It would only be a matter of days before the murderous pair struck again. Judith took herself out in search of a new victim. She drove the streets of Rome, Georgia, wanting to pick up another young girl to kill. She found the perfect victim - a woman at a payphone. The potential victim was alone and looked easily picked up; perhaps she was waiting for a lift that hadn't arrived. This is where Judith would offer her a ride and take her straight back to the motel where she and Alvin were living.

However, the woman got strange vibes from Judith. The lone woman was indeed waiting for a ride and rejected Judith's offer to take her where she needed to go. Thankfully, the woman's husband came and collected her before Judith could claim her as victim number two.

Annoyed, Judith returned to Alvin empty-handed. Still, neither she nor her deviant husband would give up the hunt. On October 4, Judith was again trawling the streets for the next captive. She saw 22-year-old Janice Chatman with her husband, John Hancock. Judith only wanted Janice but figured that Alvin would easily deal with the man. So, Lady Sundown picked up her CB radio and told Nightrider she'd found the perfect second victim. However, there was a small problem to take care of - the man she was with.

Judith pulled up beside the pair. She asked for directions to a fake destination, and Judith feigned confusion when the married couple told her the route she needed to take. She asked the couple to hop in the car and show her the way. "I'm new in town; I have no clue where to go," Judith lied. The 18-year-old claimed she'd just arrived in the area and was yet to make any friends.

The couple took pity on the lost teenager and jumped in her car. They drove for a bit, with Alvin eventually pulling up beside Judith's vehicle with their twins in tow.

Judith pulled over and introduced John Hancock and Janice Chatman to her husband and their children. The four got along, chatting and shooting the breeze before Alvin told the couple he and Judith were heading to a party nearby. Would they like to come?

The couple agreed, but Alvin suggested John come with him in his car to guide the way. Janice should stay with Judith so she wouldn't get lost, and they'd all meet up at the party. However, this was all just a ruse to separate the couple and render them vulnerable. Still, the pair agreed to Alvin's suggestion and headed out to the "party" in twos.

Along the way, John told Alvin to pull over since he needed to pee. Alvin did so, but Judith stealthily followed the man into the wooded area where he was going to relieve himself. She had her pistol in hand and, before firing shots at the victim, coldly said to him, "Don't worry, I'll take care of Janice." Judith then retreated to the car and drove Janice back to the motel room where she and Alvin lived.

Just like they'd done with Lisa, the nefarious Neelleys bound, abused, assaulted, raped, and tortured Janice. The 22-year-old victim had learning disabilities, and the callous couple had used her trusting nature for their own sick gain.

When the Neelleys were done, the pair drove Janice to a desolate area where Judith shot her in the back. This didn't prove fatal, so Alvin picked the badly injured woman up and held her against a tree, where Judith shot her point blank. The body was dumped in a nearby creek.

Meanwhile, unbeknownst to the Neelleys, John Hancock hadn't succumbed to the gun wounds inflicted upon him. He'd crawled his way out of the woodland where he was shot and managed to make it to the roadside. With all his energy spent, he had no choice but to wait for a passerby, if there was one.

Eventually, a truck driver made his way through the country road and spotted the helpless man by the roadside. He picked him up and took him to the hospital. John's nasty injuries were taken care of, and he was able to tell the police everything he knew about his attackers.

While he was awaiting his interview with the detectives assigned to the attempted murder case, John overheard a voice that sent shivers down his spine. "Y'all looking for Lisa Millican on the run from the Harpst Home?" the woman's voice said. Immediately, John recognized it as the inimitable voice of his young attacker.

By happenstance, in a room nearby, the police were listening to taped recordings of menacing calls they'd received recently. The calls were goading law enforcement and even offered the police the location of Lisa Millican's body.

Since she was deemed a "wayward" teen, the police had presumed she was a runaway. The truth of her situation became far more sinister when the caller confessed to killing the girl and tossing her into a canyon.

As the eerie phone calls were being played, John Hancock burst into the room and said, "That's the woman who shot me!"

However, the only evidence John could offer the police was identifying his attacker's voice and appearance and giving them a description of her and her husband's cars. Still, it was better than nothing.

Meanwhile, the Neelleys were free to roam the streets of Rome, Georgia, believing they'd got away with three murders. They were only two-thirds right - they had no clue that John had survived and was working with the police to track them down.

Floyd County Sheriff's Department reconciled the sinister calls from the young woman with the ones from weeks prior, which threatened the lives of youth workers. It was the same voice. Investigators worked for days to match the voice to a face. They sifted through the files of all juvenile delinquents and happened upon Judith Neelley. They showed the mugshot to John Hancock - he thought it was the woman who attacked him but couldn't be sure.

Investigations were hung up on Judith Neelley, their only viable suspect. However, tracking her down was another story. However, fate would be on their side when she and Alvin were arrested in Tennessee for trying to cash bad checks.

At this point, the Neelleys hadn't been charged with Lisa's killing, despite Judith's calls to the police advising them where a young girl's body was located. Now, though, detectives made their way to the canyon just as the caller had directed. Sure enough, when they got there, they were met with the sickening sight of Lisa Millican's body. Hanging off a random branch nearby was a bloodied pair of jeans - they were Judith's.

The net had closed in for the Neelleys. John Hancock was devastated to discover his girlfriend, Janice, had not been found by the police when they'd arrested the killer couple. It dawned on him that, more than likely, his partner had been killed. The police, too, shared this fear.

With the Neelleys in police custody, both criminals reacted differently to their arrest. Alvin got a lawyer straight away and was evasive about his part in the crimes. Judith rejected a lawyer and seemed to be forthcoming with her confessions.

Alvin claimed he feared his young wife and that their crime spree had been all her doing. He only partook out of fear. He guided the police to Janice Chatman's body. The sexual assaults inflicted upon her prior to her death were only something Alvin carried out because he feared Judith, according to him.

Judith was much less evasive and spilled everything in minute detail. She admitted attacking her former youth worker's properties but claimed she did so out of revenge. They'd raped and abused her while she was detained, allegations that were dismissed. When confronted about the murders of Lisa Millican and Janice Chatman, she admitted all: the abductions, the torture, the sexual abuse, and the eventual killings.

The Neelleys were quickly charged with the murders. With both having different accounts of their part in the sickening crimes, they suddenly turned on one another.

While in custody awaiting trial, Judith gave birth to her third child, a baby boy. All three of the 18-year-olds' children had now been born while she was detained by authorities.

Judith's appointed defense was a man named Bob French, who, after meeting his client, came away disliking her immensely. However, as all defense attorneys are trained to do, he was going to work as best he could to ensure his client got the least amount of jail time possible, regardless of their likability or clear guilt. Bob was going to try to use Judith's age to sway the jury into going down the youth offender route again. This would mean a much lighter sentence for her.

However, he knew Judith wouldn't come across well when the time came for her to take the stand at that trial. Not just because she seemed uncaring and even boastful about her crimes but because she was unkempt. Bob felt as though the jury would be less harsh if his client were pretty, pristine, and proper.

He had his work cut out. He got Judith's dental work carried out and bought her some smart attire for the trial. While he was buffing his client's veneer, he could do nothing about the wickedness beneath. He had no defense for her other than that she was just another victim of Alvin Neelley.

When the trial commenced, Bob portrayed Judith as Alvin's slave, powerless to escape him out of fear. He would beat her mercilessly, he told the court.

The prosecution would have damning evidence to counter this take, though. They'd managed to track down the woman Judith tried to pick up at the payphone. Others came forward to testify that Judith had tried to pick them up, too, and she didn't seem coerced or abused.

However, when it was his turn to take the stand, even John Hancock admitted that it seemed like Alvin was the one calling the shots. He was the one who was instigating the contact on the CB radio. He was the one who was barking directions. According to John, Alvin shouted at Judith to "hurry up" when she hesitated before shooting him.

The defense had another trick up their sleeve to help convince the jury that Alvin Neelley was a cold, coercive abuser. His ex-wife, the woman he'd left to elope with Judith, took the stand. She told the court how Alvin would abuse her, beat her, push her around while she was pregnant, and even tried to rape her younger sister. Whenever the woman tried to flee the relationship, she said Alvin would threaten to harm the children if she dared. Alvin's former wife only got her freedom when her abuser lost interest in her in favor of Judith.

The prosecution would question her honesty. They put it to her that she'd never endured a broken bone nor had her children, yet she claimed to have been in a three-year abusive relationship. This didn't ring true, they said. Such baseless tactics wouldn't be allowed in the courtroom today, but this was the early 80s, and toxic victim-blaming wasn't uncommon. Alvin's ex-wife, understandably, left the court in tears.

Eventually, Judith was brought to the stand. She was nonchalant, full of giddiness and laughter. This didn't help the jury warm to her. While her brand-new teeth and tailored clothing helped clean up the exterior, it was hard to hide the fact that Judith dimply had no remorse for the crimes she'd committed.

In a bid to explain his client's seemingly unbothered behavior, Bob asked Judith how she dealt with nervousness. She replied that she smiled when she was nervous, something she'd been doing a lot of. Bob then guided Judith in explaining her difficult childhood right up until she met the much older Alvin, who pursued her aggressively.

Bob asked Judith to explain her time with Alvin. She said he quickly became violent, and his abuse transitioned into the bedroom, too. He would become jealous for no reason and beat her if household tasks weren't done to his liking. Judith also admitted the allegations she made about the youth workers abusing her were lies, though she said Alvin encouraged her to make them up.

If you know about the Paul Bernardo and Karla Homolka crimes, you may feel that this story is beginning to mirror theirs. Paul would want young girls to rape and torture, and his willing accomplice (and wife) Karla would help him acquire them. She would also partake in the abuse. Paul would mercilessly beat Karla throughout their marriage, and there was no doubt she was often fearful of him. However, they recorded most of their crimes on a video camera, and you can see she was extremely willing to help him carry out the torture murders.

Just like the Bernardo and Homolka crimes, Judith claimed that Alvin wanted "a virgin" to tie up in their motel room. Judith would trawl the streets and look for the perfect victim to pick up. When he was done, Judith killed the women at Alvin's orders because she was afraid of him. It was them or her, she reasoned.

Bob French's closing argument was for the jury not to think of Judith as a woman whose husband "slaps her around now and then" but as a woman who was "beaten every day of her life." Again, comments like this weren't as perplexing in an '80s courtroom as they are today, though we can still mull over their ridiculousness.

The prosecution ended their argument by insisting Judith wasn't brainwashed and had never been abused by Alvin. She was, of her own accord, a cold-blooded killer.

The jury was sent away to make their decision on March 21, 1983. The next day, they had the decision firmly made - Judith Neelley was a double murderer. She was sentenced to death by electrocution, the youngest woman to be sentenced to death.

Alvin Neelley was handed two life terms in jail. He was incarcerated until his death in November 2005.

In January 1999, Judith was just days from meeting her maker when then-Governor of Alabama Fob James cut her death sentence to life in prison with the possibility of parole.

Since then, Judith has applied for parole a number of times, the most recent being in 2023. As before, it was denied. Lisa Millican's siblings attended the hearing, which Judith was not present at, and voiced their concern about her possible release. "Why keep putting families through this - she killed a child."

Their feelings embody a quote that goes along the lines of, "Giving grace to the guilty is handing cruelty to the innocent," and I can't say I disagree with them.

A Woodland Nightmare

Troubled teens are often vulnerable to the predators and nefarious monsters that live among us. Youths with troubled backgrounds and those who suffer from parental neglect are prime targets for abusers and those with violent predilections.

The tragic and utterly brutal murder of 17-year-old Hannah Windsor is one of those cases. Her killer had a similar background to her; he had ADHD and endured a troubled upbringing, just like Hannah. However, 18-year-old Adam Lewis was a far cry from the warmhearted and gregarious person Hannah was. Adam was a sadistic, cruel young man who inflicted a sickening attack on his girlfriend before killing her.

Born in Liverpool, England, in 1995, Hannah was a precocious and inquisitive child who struggled in school. A subsequent diagnosis of attention deficit hyperactivity disorder helped her teachers understand why the pupil struggled to focus in lessons. Although Hannah struggled academically, she flourished socially. She made friends with ease, chatting to whoever her teachers sat her next to, though incidentally, this also got the sociable girl in trouble.

The details surrounding Hannah's upbringing and what led to the teenager being housed in a homeless shelter are unclear, but by the age of 17, Hannah was on the authorities' radar. This included housing authorities, the police, and even her local youth offending team. Again, it's not clear why she needed the help of these agencies, but it's understood Hannah was recognized as vulnerable due to her unstable situation.

Still, she attended college, and it was here she'd meet her soon-to-be boyfriend, Adam Lewis. The pair attended a school for those with behavioral problems, though Hannah and Adam's temperaments were much different from one another. Where Hannah had difficulty focusing and paying attention, Adam struggled to socialize and "fit in." His violent tendencies likely had something to do with his inability to make friends.

Hannah was known to befriend just about everyone and eventually entered a relationship with Adam. However, after a short stint of dating, it became apparent that the relationship wasn't going to be a dreamy and romantic first love for Hannah. The pair would often break up, only to get back together days or weeks later.

The ins and outs of their relationship have never been publicized, but Adam's violent temperament and wicked nature have been. This can shed some light on why their relationship was so tumultuous.

Adam was born in 1994 to parents who, by all accounts, neglected him. The fact that Adam was found to have severe learning difficulties only compounded the bleak existence he endured as a child.

His teachers at school noticed that Adam struggled greatly with his studies, was unable to make friends, and lashed out when something upset him. More than this, it was also noted that despite Adam's lack of friendship throughout school, he didn't appear to want to make friends, either. He seemed indifferent towards others, at best, and sometimes seemed to despise his peers.

By the time Adam was nine, his parents had lost custody of the boy. They had been made aware of Adam's issues yet did nothing to help or nurture their child. He was removed from the neglectful situation and placed under the guardianship of his grandparents, who offered stability, care, and the desire to understand their grandson. However, by this point, it seems the trauma he'd endured had already molded Adam into the young adult he would become: uncaring, sadistic, and violent.

By age 11, Adam would rebel despite his grandparents' care and concern for the boy. He began drinking alcohol. He even began setting fires for fun. It was clear that Adam didn't have the ability to contemplate or think before he acted, which is something we begin to develop at the age of six. The idea of consequence is generally ingrained by age 13. This wasn't the case for Adam. He did what he wanted regardless of the outcome. This trait would remain a constant in his young life.

The teachers at his school struggled to manage the boy and his outbursts. In the end, it was agreed they didn't have the means to educate him, so plans were made for him to attend a school for those with behavioral issues.

Adam and Hannah met at the school some years before they began dating. In late 2011, the pair made it official. Adam was around 17 years old when they began dating, with the mental age of a ten or 11-year-old.

Adam's violent and reckless behavior was rapidly getting out of control. In May 2012, he broke into his sister's ex's house, stealing items of value to sell. Before exiting the ransacked property, he set multiple fires, which caused a lot of damage to the house. Adam didn't think - or, rather, didn't care - about the lives he'd endangered by setting the blaze. The fire almost spread to neighboring properties, but the fire department was called just in time to stop the flames from reaching any other homes.

After looting the house and setting it ablaze, Adam quickly realized he would be suspect number one for the crime. He figured the police would be after him within a matter of hours, so to avoid arrest, he made plans to camp out in the woods. The authorities wouldn't find him there, he figured, and set up camp at a scenic wooded spot called Bidston Hill.

He brought along all the essentials he'd need to survive for a while, including a Swiss army knife. When he was settled in his temporary home, he rang Hannah, whom he'd just recently gotten back together with after yet another acrimonious separation. During the phone call, Adam confessed to his girlfriend that he had ransacked and set alight his sister's ex-boyfriend's home. Though shocked at his admission, Hannah still agreed to meet Adam at his campsite in the woods in the coming days.

The revelation troubled Hannah, and she knew she had to do something with the confession. After sitting on it for a short while, she told the police everything her boyfriend had admitted, although it wasn't surprising to the police. Adam was the main - only, in fact - suspect in the arson. Still, Hannah didn't reveal her partner's location to the police, perhaps preferring to tell her boyfriend to his face that she'd been speaking with investigators.

Hannah's meeting with the officers lasted a few hours, and before she departed the station, the police warned her against visiting her boyfriend. He was dangerous and violent, they told her, and the best thing she could do would be to walk away from the relationship for her own safety. She was also handed a card with a phone number on it and was told to ring it if she had any more evidence or needed anything.

Despite the warning from the police, on May 16, Hannah made her way to see Adam.

What happened next is unclear, as the only person who can tell the story is Adam Lewis, and he has never opened up about his sickening attack on Hannah. Grotesque and macabre clues left behind are the only things available to piece the grim story together.

It seems at some point during the meeting, Adam discovered that Hannah had been speaking to the police. She may have told Adam this herself, or it could have been he found the card with the investigator's number on it. The card was found at the campsite, ripped to shreds. This discovery triggered Adam to launch a vile, prolonged attack on Hannah.

He pummeled her with his fists, beating her badly before removing her clothes and tying her to a nearby tree so she was unable to move any of her limbs. The abuse resumed and escalated from this point, which saw the sick teenager force himself upon Hannah. She was unable to scream - he'd wrapped tape around her mouth.

Then, Adam retrieved his Swiss army knife and used the sharp tool to mutilate his victim's crotch. This was the start of a torturous assault on Hannah using the knife, which primarily focused on her private areas. The wicked teen caused a number of internal injuries to his girlfriend, causing her to bleed heavily.

The knife was also used to inflict awful injuries to Hannah's breasts. In another twisted act, he stuck the knife as deep as he could into her leg before dragging it down her flesh as far as he could. The girl was bleeding out. Still, at this point, if Adam had somehow, someway, gained a conscience, some empathy, or some basic regard for human life other than his own, Hannah could have been saved.

Instead, he mutilated her for hours.

Hannah survived this agonizing period of torture although it must have felt like days. Tied to a tree, stripped of her clothing, and an evil knife-wielding monster before her, she must have known her time was coming to an end. Either she would bleed out, or Adam would snuff out her life with the knife.

Instead, Adam chose to strangle Hannah to death. He tied a cord around her neck and pulled it tightly.

Once she'd succumbed to the garrote, Adam again resumed his attack on the body. Even after her death, the twisted teen felt the desire to stab and mutilate the corpse further. It's not been proven that he sexually abused Hannah again after her murder, but it's been suggested. I wouldn't be shocked if that were the case.

When Adam was done, he cut his victim from the tree and buried her under some twigs, leaves, and soil. A crude grave made by a perverted killer who was willing to let this be his former girlfriend's final resting place.

After committing the heinous crime, Adam returned to his tent and fell asleep.

The next day, he awoke to see a man walking in the sun-dappled woodland. The unsuspecting man was taking in the beauty and serenity of the woods, unaware of the horrors that were mere meters away from him. Adam walked over to the man and struck up a conversation, not something that came naturally to the teenager. This can be seen by one of the things he asked the man: how long would an 18-year-old get in jail if they'd murdered someone?

No remorse for his actions, no concern for his victim in her final moment, just pure selfishness and self-preservation from Adam.

It took two days for Hannah to be reported missing to the police. Naturally, Adam was suspect number one.

However, his apprehension wouldn't be a smooth one. Sure enough, the killer was arrested, but not for Hannah's murder. The burglary and arson attack caught up with him, and Adam was arrested on May 18 for the crimes.

He was found sleeping rough, not at the campsite, and a police check found that he was wanted for the arson attack. When the police brought him in, Adam was even wearing shoes he'd stolen in the robbery. Macabrely, they were covered in Hannah Windsor's blood. These things were overlooked, and after a few hours of being locked up and interviewed, Adam was released on bail.

After being freed, Adam visited his sister and confessed to her that he was responsible for Hannah's disappearance. Sickened by the admission, she told her grandparents, who swiftly called the police on their grandson. Adam was arrested shortly thereafter.

The police managed to get a confession out of Adam, and they requested he guide them to Hannah's body. The teenager complied, and investigators were naturally disturbed when they dug up the victim. They knew he'd killed her, but Adam hadn't told them about the sick acts of mutilation he'd carried out.

Hannah's family was able to have a funeral, which wasn't just attended by relatives and friends but heartbroken members of the community. The teenager's favorite color was pink, so to honor Hannah, some attendees chose to wear the bright color she adored.

Adam's story to the police was see-through. He said Hannah had attacked him and that's why he lashed out and killed her. This flimsy excuse couldn't answer the question, though, as to why Hannah had been sexually assaulted, tortured, and mutilated prior to her death. This wasn't a knee-jerk attack or a violent lashing out. It was slow, violent, methodical, calculated, and remorseless.

At his trial, he pleaded not guilty to murder.

A psychiatric report concluded that Adam had a very low IQ and a personality disorder but asserted that neither of these things contributed to his killing of Hannah Windsor.

At the last minute, Adam changed his plea to guilty. He admitted to two counts of sexual assault and brutal murder but declined to offer an explanation as to why he did these things.

He was handed at least 22 years behind bars.

At the sentencing hearing, the judge told Adam he "must have known what dreadful pain" Hannah was in as he tortured her, leading him to label the killing motivated by sexual and sadistic elements.

Hannah's mother, Gaynor, said the sentencing meant the family "could now find peace."

She said she felt Adam deserved the sentence he got and that justice was served. It was a stoic, composed, and admirable view from the bereft mother and one I found myself contemplating. Could I be consoled by a 22-year sentence for the individual who tortured and murdered my daughter?

I deduced that, should anyone find themselves in this tragic situation, they are likely to adjust and do what they must to survive the anguish. Wanting ten minutes in a room alone with Adam was never going to happen (as would be many a mother's want in a situation like this), so accepting that some justice was served is perhaps the only way to continue living with some semblance of sanity.

Adam Lewis could, theoretically, be back on the streets by the time he's 50 years old.

Deranged Dad

It's easy to forget that sadistic killers and evil abusers are always someone's son, brother, or father. We often don't consider that they have people who love them, and these people can't possibly imagine them to be capable of committing such atrocities as murder or sexual assault.

Despite frequently being depicted as loners with no human connection, killers often have families and loved ones.

In the case I'm about to cover, Clarence Butterfield was part of your typical American family. He had a wife, a son, and a daughter. Though, he wouldn't appreciate this as a blessing, nor would he treat his family with any kind of respect, let alone kindness.

Clarence and Catherine married in 1983 in Orange County, California. Despite Butterfield being a cruel and domineering husband, their daughter Rebekah was born in 1984. The birth of his first child didn't soften the abusive man, and his menacing ways trickled down to his infant child.

His abuse of Catherine escalated as the years went by. In one cruel incident, Butterfield tied his wife up so she couldn't run away and found her in a drum filled with ice.

Butterfield's second child was born in 1988, this time a son they named Jedidiah. Again, the man's oppressive ways remained.

A move to Las Vegas in the mid-90s did little to quell his violent outbursts. They changed the location but not the situation, which was an incredibly dangerous one: the mother and children were living with a ticking time bomb of a man whose aggression knew no bounds.

For years, Catherine endured her husband's abuse out of fear for her and her children's safety. To stay was paradoxically safer than leaving. Plus, despite the abuse he doled out, young Rebekah loved her father. However, after years of being a verbal and physical punchbag, Catherine found the courage to leave at the beginning of 2004. She urged her children to leave with her, which Jedidiah eventually did. Rebekah, however, chose to stay with her father.

This choice, born out of love and loyalty, would prove fatal. Rebekah's unwavering allegiance toward her father was repaid with violence and cruelty.

That summer, Butterfield dialed 911 and made a panicked call to the police. His home had been burglarized, he said, and his 20-year-old daughter had been harmed by the assailants. They'd stabbed Rebekah, and she needed urgent medical treatment.

Rebekah was rushed to the hospital, and Clarence told the police everything he knew about the attackers. However, the story didn't add up. It was suspicious at best, and eventually, the father admitted he was the one who'd inflicted the stab wounds on his daughter's thigh. It was an accident, he claimed. So, Rebekah was discharged from the hospital and sent back to live with her father. No further action was taken.

I'd likely not be here writing this chapter if it had been. At least, not recounting Rebekah's death; perhaps some other poor soul would have fallen victim to Clarence Butterfield's temperament.

Rebekah still maintained contact with her mother and brother during this time, though she still declined to live with them. In a meeting in 2005 with Jed, Rebekah turned up lethargic and seemingly fearful. Jedidiah didn't notice his sister having any noticeable injuries, but he knew as well as anyone that their father wasn't just physically abusive. When the siblings parted ways, the concerned younger brother had no way of knowing it would be the last time he'd see his sister again.

After two years of living alone with her father, Rebekah was sent to the emergency room for the second time. By this point, the father and daughter had moved back to California, further separating her from her mother and brother. The hospital visit saw Rebekah require an x-ray on her left leg, which revealed some shocking findings for the doctors. The most prominent being the bullet lodged in her ankle.

Still, she received the necessary treatment and returned home.

Toward the end of 2006, the father and daughter bought a motorhome to live in. They parked up on one of Butterfield's friend's properties free of charge. Rebekah was often seen around the home, doing housework or taking the trash out. Butterfield's friend noted that the young girl had a funny walk, something he questioned the father about. "She was in a bad car accident," Clarence lied. The friend didn't dig much deeper.

To help make ends meet, Rebekah worked at a home improvement store. In December 2006, she wouldn't show up for her shift, something that was unlike the hardworking young woman. Around the same time, Butterfield's friend noticed Rebekah's absence from the motorhome. She was always moseying around, even if she did look somber most of the time.

If anyone asked Butterfield where his daughter had gone, he told them she'd gone to Las Vegas to live with her mother.

Rebekah had simply vanished off the face of the earth, but nobody was looking for her.

Jed came and visited his father—one of the few visits he made—in 2007. His sister was noticeably absent. When Jedidiah asked his father where Rebekah was, his response was vague. At one point, the unbothered dad said his young daughter had moved to another country to live with an unknown love interest. When this didn't quell Jedidiah's questions and prompted him to probe his father for more details, Butterfield then came up with another reason Rebekah wasn't around.

His next excuse would be laughable if the tale weren't so tragic. He said Rebekah had been eaten by sharks.

Unsurprisingly, Jed wasn't satisfied with the answers, or lack thereof, he was getting from his father, so he returned to Las Vegas. It's unclear what the confused young man told Catherine about her daughter's whereabouts, but perhaps fear prevented her from confronting her abusive ex about it.

The following year, in 2008, Clarence Butterfield would just about admit he'd done something terrible to a fellow churchgoer. He asked his acquaintance to think of the worst thing humanly possible, to which the man replied, "killing someone." Butterfield then alluded to the fact that he'd done the worst thing a human could do before asking him to keep the conversation private.

That summer, Butterfield also made a (almost) full confession to another churchgoer, admitting he'd killed someone. He omitted the fact that he'd killed his own daughter, and not in a quick, merciless way either. He told the shocked woman that he hid the body in his freezer.

Neither churchgoer did anything with the disturbing information they were given.

Around the same time, Catherine was becoming increasingly anxious about Rebekah's whereabouts. Her daughter hadn't been in touch, and there were no postcards from her supposed time abroad. Surely the tale about being a victim of a shark attack wasn't true?

Catherine bit the bullet and called her ex husband for answers. She got an entirely new story - Rebekah had drowned while surfing abroad. Devastated and unable to, quite rightly, simply accept his story, Catherine called the police.

Subsequently, law enforcement tried to contact Butterfield, but he refused to cooperate. He would hang up on their calls and refuse to answer his door. Officers posted letters through his door and requested he call them or visit the police station, neither of which he did. This was not the action of a concerned father, but law enforcement didn't have anything to arrest the man for.

For months after Catherine's call to the police, Butterfield successfully evaded the police. Until the September of that year, when he was arrested for writing bad checks. He was thrown in jail, where he got friendly with another inmate.

His newfound friend was just days away from release, and Butterfield had a favor to ask him. In exchange for his one and only possession, the motorhome, he wanted the convict to get rid of a freezer he had stored in there. Butterfield claimed that the 5-foot-long freezer only had some dead fish inside it, but he wanted it gone. If his friend did that for him, the vehicle was his.

A strange request, although one that the criminal was unable to carry out. The police got there before him.

They opened up the ominous-looking freezer that had been tied tightly with tape. They cut the wrappings of sticky tape to reveal a heavy object wrapped in a number of plastic bags. The body-shaped object was also wrapped in lashings of tape and secured by rope. Sure enough, when the bags were cut off and pulled away from the object, it was discovered to be a dead body. The woman's limbs had been tied, her arms secured behind her back. Her body was riddled with bullets.

Clarence Butterfield's motorhome offered a plethora of evidence to suggest he was the culprit. A revolver was found in his belongings, along with other weapons and ammo.

The dead body was quickly found to be that of Rebekah Butterfield. Her autopsy tragically showed the horrors she endured before she died.

Her legs were filled with bullets and shrapnel. Her right thigh, leg, and foot all had bullets lodged in the flesh. The shots were determined not to have been fatal. They were, however, believed to have been a method of torture from the assailant, strongly believed by this point to be her father.

The reason for the shots to the leg wasn't to kill; it was to cause pain and fear for the victim. The victim had been tied up, and the marks left behind suggest she struggled to break free of her restraints. Sickeningly, she'd also been shot in the head, with the bullet grazing her skin. Again, this was likely to cause as much fear and torment for Rebekah as possible.

The torture had been prolonged, just like her death. She was stuffed in the freezer while she was still alive and slowly asphyxiated to death. Rebekah was bound at the hands and feet, making her escape impossible. The five minutes it took her to die would have been agonizing.

Armed with the pathologist's evidence, the police went to Butterfield for answers. They were certain he was the culprit but needed him to flesh out what had happened. Most of all — although there would never be a satisfying answer to this — they wanted to know why he'd done this to his daughter.

But he denied involvement. He admitted he'd found his daughter lying dead after a fall in the shower. To preserve her body, he placed her in the freezer. When the police found Rebekah's body, she was naked, although Butterfield, for whatever reason, asserted that she was fully clothed when he locked her in the freezer. How she suddenly became naked was a question he couldn't answer.

When the father was asked why he chose to freeze his daughter instead of calling 911, he said he wanted to conserve her corpse on the off chance that, one day, revival was possible. It seems the father didn't care if his story was believable or not, he simply wanted to abolish himself of all guilt.

Due to the sheer unbelievability of Butterfield's story, he was sent for psychological evaluation. He was found to be of sound mind. Therefore, he was fit to stand trial for the torture murder of his daughter. Despite all of the evidence against him, the 55-year-old denied killing Rebekah.

The prosecution also brought up the possibility of Butterfield sexually abusing Rebekah. They considered questioning him about it when he took the stand but ultimately decided not to. The basis for the suspicion of this type of abuse was, allegedly, the disgraced father had told friends that Rebekah wasn't his daughter. He followed that up with a comment about "doing things with her that nobody would do with their daughter."

For the torture and murder of his daughter, Clarence Butterfield got life behind bars.

To think that, if he hadn't been arrested for writing bad checks, Rebekah may never have been found is a frightening notion. She lay cold and alone in a freezer for 22 months, and it seems as though Butterfield was considering disposing of her at some point. Had he done so, a conviction would unlikely have been made.

For her unwavering loyalty to her father, Rebekah Butterfield was rewarded with an untimely and brutal death. To this day, Clarence Butterfield refuses to admit his guilt.

Serve and Protect

If you're from the UK, you may already know about the case I'm covering in this chapter. It caused uproar, protests, and much debate about the safety of women at the hands of men. Still, despite this case being rather high-profile in the UK, it's not widely known elsewhere.

Due to its social impact and the number of true crime followers worldwide who don't know about the case, I've chosen to include it in this volume. This is the story of Sarah Everard and her murder at the hands of an off-duty police officer.

Sarah Everard was born in 1987 in Surrey, South East England. The family moved to York, where the youngster grew up. Sarah was a bright girl who was exceptionally close to her family and a natural when it came to making friends. After leaving high school, she attended Durham University to earn a degree in human geography. This qualification allowed her to move to London, where she got a job as a marketing executive. She lived in the bustling area of Brixton Hill, which is famed for its nightlife and popular street markets.

On the night of March 3, 2021, Sarah was making her way home from a friend's house in Clapham to her home in Brixton. It was a clear, cool night, and Sarah chose to walk instead of getting a taxi. The walk was simple and well-lit. She set off at around 9 p.m. and should have been home just before 10. She never made it home.

As she made the journey home, she called her boyfriend, and the pair spoke until 9:30 p.m. She would be home shortly and let him know she'd arrived safely, she told him. When the text to say she was home didn't arrive, her boyfriend got concerned. When Sarah didn't show up to a client meeting the following morning, further worry arose. When she wasn't replying to any texts and calls, friends and family knew something was wrong.

On March 4, almost 24 hours since he'd last spoken to her, Sarah's boyfriend went to her flat, but nobody was answering. The anxiety he felt turned to dread. He called the police.

Sarah wouldn't just vanish. She had no reason to, she had never hinted at packing up and leaving everything behind, and ignoring texts and calls was unlike Sarah. Whatever had happened to her, wherever she had gone, friends and family had to swallow the idea that she didn't go there willingly. Something sinister had happened.

Immediately, the case became headline news in the UK. Posters were put up in and around the area where she was last seen. She was caught on a doorbell camera around 15-20 minutes from her home. She'd almost made it. After that, she just vanished.

Of course, nobody just vanishes.

Local rescue teams searched ponds, officers trawled nearby parks, and visited nearby houses. Her family put out an appeal, which resulted in over 100 calls from the public, which yielded no results. Still, her loved ones remained hopeful about the outcome."We just need to get her home," they said in their statement. It was clear they believed she was alive.

The hope and optimism they felt at such an anxiety-riddled, agonizing time is admirable. The reality, however, was heartbreaking: Sarah was already dead. Not only that, her killer was someone who'd sworn to respect and protect civilians: police constable Wayne Couzens.

Wayne Couzens was born in December 1972 in Kent, South East England. He left school at 16 and took up work in a car garage. Life as a mechanic wasn't what Wayne envisioned for himself, and his dream job was to be a police officer. He made four years' worth of applications before finally getting the constable job in 2006.

Over the next few years, he flitted from department to department, becoming a firearms officer before eventually joining the Metropolitan Police as a constable. He then transferred to the Parliamentary and Diplomatic Protection Department, which specialized in protecting government premises, such as Downing Street and Westminster.

However, this role should never have been made available to him. Wayne hadn't carried out the required two-year probation period with the Metropolitan Police before he joined the Parliamentary and Diplomatic Protection Department. Not only that, the required vetting for his role was also not carried out.

Just days before Sarah's disappearance, Wayne had booked a hire car despite already owning a car of his own. After work on March 3, he went and retrieved the vehicle before driving around London, seemingly without aim.

He was caught on CCTV in several areas during the course of the night, including Earls Court and Clapham. Just after 9 pm, he drove past a young woman walking alone.

It was Sarah Everard.

The following timeline is pieced together by the evidence the police collected in the aftermath of Sarah's disappearance.

At 9:34 pm, he pulled up beside Sarah and got out of the car. He showed her his police warrant and cuffed her. Since it was early 2021, restrictions were still in place amidst the global virus outbreak, so it could have been that the off-duty officer used her flouting of these rules as a reason to arrest her. Sarah complied despite having done nothing wrong. After all, he was a police officer. He wouldn't harm her.

CCTV captured the hire car, with Sarah in the back, at various points as it headed toward Kent.

Just over two hours after picking her up, Wayne Couzens bundled her from the hire car and into his personal vehicle. Shortly thereafter, they stopped in a small village area, proven by his phone signal connecting to nearby towers. This, it's believed, is where he raped Sarah.

He killed her by wrapping his police belt around her neck until she died.

After the brutal attack and subsequent murder, the man drove to a gas station with the dead victim in the car and then took her to a plot of land he owned. Here, he is believed to have disposed of the body while he returned the rental car the following morning. He then got rid of Sarah's phone by throwing it into some water.

It seems his vile actions caused Wayne to panic. He called his boss to tell him he felt under stress and didn't go to work in the days after the crime. He even told his superior that he no longer wanted to carry a firearm.

While off work, Wayne returned to the plot of land he'd dumped Sarah on. Her body was encased inside an old fridge, which he then set alight. He placed her remains in a polypropylene bag and threw it into a nearby pond.

Wayne must have known the police were onto him. He was acting erratically, and he didn't exactly do a good job of being inconspicuous about the sick crime he'd committed. Even with him trying to wipe the trail clean by using a hire car and burning the body beyond recognition, he'd certainly left more than a trail of breadcrumbs for officers to follow.

Namely, the police had now had the chance to review much of the CCTV footage that was available to them. Not only that, there had been witnesses who'd seen the man handcuffing Sarah and guiding her into the back of his car. A couple were driving by, but they thought the woman had done something wrong and was really under arrest.

Unbeknown to the killer, a camera had picked him up as she stood next to the hire car, talking to his soon-to-be victim. He had his arm stretched out, showing her his warrant.

After days of panic and contemplating what to do, Wayne attempted to wipe all data from his cell phone. His aim to remove any clues proved futile; there was CCTV footage of him and the hire car he'd been driving, which was booked in his name. So, the police arrested him on March 9 under suspicion of kidnapping Sarah.

However, there was no body and, thus, no DNA evidence to link back to the suspect. He was questioned for hours, and at first, he denied recognizing Sarah when he was shown pictures of her. By this point, pictures of her had been all over national television and on flyers and newspaper boards all around the country. Pretty much everyone with a TV and a working cell phone knew what Sarah looked like; she was front page news. Still, Wayne insisted he didn't recognize her.

Eventually, the amount of evidence that suggested he'd "arrested" her on March 3 must have weighed too heavily for him to continue his lie of not knowing who Sarah was. He finally confessed to kidnapping the young woman but insisted that he'd left her very much alive and well. This "confession," though, was see-through.

The man claimed that he'd been having money troubles ever since he got mixed up with an Eastern European gang. According to Wayne, he'd used a sex worker weeks prior to kidnapping Sarah and underpaid her since he didn't have enough cash. This angered the sex workers' bosses, who tracked Wayne down and demanded that he "obtain another woman" for them.

The gang would hurt his family if Wayne didn't do as they demanded. The European men were apparently watching him from outside his house.

So, he kidnapped Sarah Everard and drove her out of London as requested. Then, a van with Romanian number plates flashed him, so he pulled over. Three men got out of the van and threw Sarah in the back. She was alive and uninjured at this point, Wayne said.

Knowing what we know now, this exposes how heartless the man is: to want to allow Sarah's family to believe she was still alive is beyond comprehension. Should his paper-thin lies have been believed, Sarah's family would potentially have still, to this day, believed she was out there somewhere.

Days passed, and the police were still looking for the woman's body. Rivers, woods, and rural areas were all inspected with a fine tooth comb to no avail. The tiny bit of hope her loved ones had was diminishing. Then, on March 10, the devastating discovery was made. Sarah's incinerated body was found in a bag around 100 meters from land that Wayne owned.

She had to be identified by her dental records.

Wayne was subsequently charged with her murder. While in custody, the day after his murder arrest, he suffered an injury to his head. It's unclear what happened, but he had to be hospitalized for it. A police statement said the injury happened while Wayne was by himself in his cell.

Initially, Wayne only pleaded guilty to the kidnapping and rape of Sarah, though he would eventually plead guilty to her murder, too. On September 29, 2021, he was given a whole life tariff behind bars.

After his arrest, more revelations of Wayne Couzens's history of sick acts made news headlines.

In November 2020, while on duty, he walked toward a female cyclist in a wooded area while performing an act on himself.

Less than a month before he murdered Sarah, on February 14, he ordered food from a drive-thru and, while at the payment window, pulled his pants down to expose himself to the shocked cashier. A fortnight later, he did the same thing at the exact same establishment.

The fast food restaurant contacted the police about the indecent exposure. The man had used his own credit card for the transactions, and the manager had managed to capture CCTV footage of the vehicle the flasher was driving. It clearly showed the number plate. Wayne had used his personal vehicle while committing the perverse act.

On the day Sarah was abducted, a female officer visited the fast food place to investigate the complaints. Despite being given all the information and evidence the manager had collated, the officer didn't trace the car back to Wayne. After his crimes came to light, she was sacked by the Metropolitan Police.

Other officers' gross misconduct was also uncovered after Wayne's arrest. The killer cop was part of a group chat, and their texts got leaked to the press. The conversation included joking about rape and engaging in sexual acts with victims of domestic violence (who, according to one of the officers, "loved" being beaten up). The same officer commented that he "raped a bystander" while on shift. Wayne Couzens also used racist language in the messages.

As a result of the leaked messages, six officers lost their jobs, two of whom were jailed for their part in the twisted group chat.

The aftermath of Sarah's murder left the UK in a state of anger and fear. A promising young woman's life was snuffed out by a police officer — the very person a lone woman would look to for help if she ran into trouble. It turned out that Wayne Couzens *was* the trouble.

This then caused the Metropolitan Police to cease deploying singular plain-clothed police officers. Still, this did little to quell the unease that engulfed the UK. More incidents involving Wayne Couzens's past behavior came to light, including other incidents of exposure that the police didn't investigate properly.

On another occasion, a sex worker made her way to the police station demanding to see him, claiming lack of payment for her services. He was also reported to have assaulted a drag queen in 2018. A popular radio host also went on record to say she'd been a victim of Couzens's indecent exposure 13 years prior. She reported the crime to the police at the time but claimed they "laughed at her."

As the months passed, the British public was still dissatisfied with the way the police had dealt with the criminal and seemingly let him get away with so much before he finally murdered an innocent woman. In response, in September 2021, the Metropolitan Police issued a statement that further angered the baying public. They suggested that should a woman be approached by a single police officer and feel uncomfortable, they should shout to a passerby or run to a nearby house.

It seemed that, even months after the disturbing event of Sarah's murder, they laid the responsibility firmly on the shoulders of the would-be victims.

This feeling was reiterated when the North Yorkshire Police Commissioner said women needed to be more "streetwise." Calls were made for him to resign, which he initially declined to do. The backlash was too great for him to regain the public's trust, though, and he eventually resigned.

The feelings of the public, particularly women, were yet again misunderstood when the UK government announced they'd inject millions in funding into the police force. The public's issue was that the horrific murder was carried out by a police officer — extra funding wouldn't ensure they could trust the officers who approached them.

In the years since Sarah Everard's murder, more stories of crooked cops have come to light.

In a more recent case, 24-year-old Cliff Mitchell, a Metropolitan Police officer, was found guilty of a sickening spate of sex attacks. These included thirteen counts of rape, three of which involved a person under 13. He was also found guilty of kidnap.

In September 2023, he raped a woman at knifepoint. Afterward, he took his sweatshirt off and used it to blindfold her. He then used cable ties to bind her wrists and bundled her into his car. Eventually, the woman was able to escape the vehicle and flagged down a woman who let her in her car.

Mitchell was later arrested, and he was found guilty of this assault. The case also prompted a 2017 rape allegation toward the attacker to be reponed, which was closed years prior. This time around, he was charged with the attack and jailed.

Then there's the case of David Carrick, a Metropolitan police officer who raped at least 12 women over 17 years. He believed his job title made him "untouchable." The 48-year-old was arrested in October 2021 when one of his victims reported that she had been raped by him. The recent murder of Sarah Everard had prompted the woman to muster the courage to report her abuser.

The news spread and more women came forward, each with their own story. None of the women knew each other, but each of the 13 women had an eerily similar tale to tell. Carrick had met some women via dating apps, others he met while working.

He became a police officer in 2001, roughly around the time his offending began. Over the course of his career in the police, a number of women reported him and made complaints about his behavior. Nothing was done with this information.

Carrick would often refer to his job as a police officer while carrying out the rapes and would even hold his police-issued gun while carrying out the attacks. The sick man would remind his victims that he was "the boss." He would deter his victims from going to the police, reminding them he was a serving officer and that nobody would believe them. "I am the law," he would say.

In total, Carrick was charged with 85 offenses and was found guilty of them all, which led to him receiving 36 life sentences. He will serve a minimum of 30 years in jail. It turns out he was *not* the law.

These cases are just a small handful of "crooked cop" or "killer cop" cases that have come to light in recent years. It's a frightening notion that certain police officers — who swear an oath to protect us — have felt able to hide behind their status as law enforcement to carry out heinous crimes.

The "Friendly" Neighborhood Monster

Despite Nathaniel Bar-Jonah's intimidating stature — he weighed more than 300 pounds, donned a wiry mustache, and had a stern, downturned face — he was a well-liked and respected member of the Great Falls community in Montana.

Few people knew just how sinister and evil the man truly was. The only people who were aware of Nathaniel's dark side were the vulnerable and the voiceless within the community: the children.

Born David Paul Brown in 1957, the youngster was raised in Worcester, Massachusetts. The boy was known to have an insatiable hunger, going as far as crying non-stop unless he was being fed. As a result, the child quickly gained weight, and with young David being so inactive, this rapidly turned into obesity. He became immobile for a period, during which he was so heavy neither his mother nor father could lift him.

As he grew up, the boy's father was incredibly strict with him. David was beaten frequently by dad Philip, who was fearful his son would grow up to be homosexual. It's unclear what made Philip feel this way or why he felt beating his son would abolish any innate feelings he may have had, but it appears young David was singled out by his father.

Despite the threat of violence, David would still regularly misbehave as he grew up; he would often steal toys and food from other children and take his sibling's belongings. For these misgivings, he would be lashed with a leather belt by his dad.

The child was clearly troubled and displayed plenty of strange behavior despite his young age. His concerning behavior wasn't dealt with by his parents in the right way. He was simultaneously mistreated and spoiled. He was beaten for small infractions yet was given most things he asked for.

Certainly, when the boy asked for an Ouija board for his seventh birthday, he got it. Most seven-year-olds don't wish to summon the dead, but David Brown wasn't like most seven-year-olds.

The boy didn't have any friends to try the board out with, though. So, he decided to head out onto the street and scope out the neighborhood kids. A 5-year-old girl caught his eye, and David headed over and told the girl he had an Ouija board that could look into the future. He asked if she would help him use it, and the intrigued girl agreed. They headed down to the Brown family basement, but David had no intentions of looking into the future. Instead, he attacked the girl, his hands wrapped around her neck, trying to strangle her.

The shrieking emanating from the basement caught David's mother's attention. She raced down the stairs to see her son on top of the terrified child. While the woman managed to pull her son from the little girl, she barely reprimanded her boy for his unacceptable behavior. It was just David being David, after all.

A few years later, David lured a six-year-old boy to a desolate snow-filled area under the guise of sledding. The teen sexually assaulted the boy before letting him go.

By the age of 15, David's behavior hadn't improved. In fact, it only got more sinister. With the benefit of age, the boy became even more wily and sneaky in carrying out his criminal behavior. The teen concocted a plan to write a letter—made up of letters cut from magazines, much like a ransom note—and sent it to two young boys. The note offered the youngsters money as a reward for following its instructions to go to the cemetery.

The boys' mother intervened, and the letter was traced back to David. Still, the police weren't involved, and David saw this as a green light to resume his troubling behavior.

The following year, in 1974, the teenager really indulged in his twisted desires in a much more conniving way. He obtained a police officer's outfit and used his disguise to abduct an 8-year-old boy as he made his way to school. By a stroke of luck, a neighbor was looking out of their window as the boy was lured away and placed into a car by the "officer" and called the police. A search for the child ensued, with the police on the lookout for the make and model of car the witness had observed the boy getting into.

Thankfully, later that day, a car matching the description of the suspect's car was reported in a parking lot. The driver had made sure to park well away from other vehicles, further making it suspicious. When the police arrived, they found David Brown in the car. In the back was the young boy they were searching for. The condition officers found him in was sickening.

He was covered in his own urine and feces, having been clearly terrified at the ordeal he'd endured. The child had been assaulted in the worst ways imaginable by the culprit. Fortunately, he was now safe, thanks in no small part to the quick-thinking neighbor who'd spotted the abduction.

For this sickening crime, David Brown was given a few months probation. Again, it seems the lack of consequence or punishment only bolstered his ability to carry out horrific attacks as he pleased. The next — inevitable — attack on a youngster was just days before his probation period ended.

A nine-year-old girl fell victim to Brown after he yet again donned a fake police officer uniform and demanded she get in the car. He drove her to a desolate area where he raped her. The sick fiend threw the girl out of the car when she began to vomit and convulse. As he flung his victim from the vehicle, a bystander noticed the shocking event and jotted down the number plate.

Brown was arrested for this second offense, but in a twist of injustice, nothing came of it. Naturally, the monster wasn't going to stop now; so far there had been zero repercussions for his evil actions. In fact, his criminal offending was only just beginning.

In September of 1974, Brown yet again pretended to be law enforcement to entice children into his vehicle. This time, he pretended to be an FBI agent, and his ruse saw him pluck two young boys from the street as they walked home from the cinema in Shrewsbury, Massachusetts.

Brown drove them to a desolate area and came prepared with handcuffs. The fact that he quite clearly planned these attacks shows just how calculated, dangerous, and evil he was. While his other attacks on children were sickening, he would amp up his level of violence on his two new victims.

With each boy handcuffed, Brown set about torturing them. When the savage man was done, he jumped on the chest of one of the boys repeatedly. Bear in mind that Brown was around 375 pounds by this point, and he put the entire force of his body into the jumps. Once he was sure the boy was dead, he flung the second boy, who was still alive, into the car and drove off.

However, the boy whom Brown had mercilessly attacked had, somehow, still clung to life. In agony, he awoke from the severe beating and sought help.

The police were informed, and once again, David Brown was arrested with another young victim in his car. Thankfully, the second boy had also survived the attack, though no doubt with many emotional scars.

Yet again, Brown was arrested for his perverse attacks on children. This time, the law wasn't so lenient on him, and he was handed a maximum of 22 years in jail. Still nowhere near what a lot of us would call true justice, but at the very least, it would offer Brown treatment for his deranged sexual desires. Not to mention, it would keep the perverse man off the streets for two decades.

However, after his stint in therapy due to him being classed as a sexually dangerous offender, this sentence was lengthened to be indefinite. He'd divulged some of his twisted fantasies to his therapist, who then decided Brown was still too dangerous to be allowed back on the streets, let alone anywhere near children. After all, one of his fantasies involved dissecting and eating his victims, an act he'd not yet carried out.

You may think the story ends here, that Brown is still locked behind bars due to the clear threat he poses to children.

Amazingly, that's not the case.

In 1991, after more psychiatric evaluations, he was deemed not to be a dangerous threat to youngsters. As such, he was released on probation. One of the recommendations of his probation was that he see a psychiatrist, though this was not mandatory. And so, a sadistic predator was once again on the streets in the summer of '91.

Prior to his release, Brown changed his legal name to Nathaniel Bar-Jonah. His reasoning for this, according to Bar-Jonah at the time, was that he wanted to know what it felt like to be discriminated against like the Jewish people.

The predator was free for all but a month before he struck again.

While stalking the streets in broad daylight, as Bar-Jonah so brazenly did, he spotted a seven-year-old boy sitting in a car alone. The perverse man couldn't find it in him to simply walk by and let the innocent child be; he had to do him some harm. So, he opened the car door and began smothering him, putting his entire body weight onto the small child.

The boy couldn't breathe, nor could he move the large man who had inexplicably taken it upon himself to sit on him.

Thankfully, passersby saw what was happening. It could have been incredibly easy for bystanders to have missed the assault taking place altogether. To those without an eagle eye, it would have just looked like Bar-Jonah was sitting in the passenger seat alone.

When people intervened, Bar-Jonah fled the scene. The witnesses and the young boy were able to give the police his description. It didn't take the officers long to figure out who they were looking for. There was only one heavyset, mustached man in the area who couldn't resist bothering children: David Brown, aka Nathaniel Bar-Jonah. He was quickly arrested again.

He couldn't deny he was the culprit. But, Bar-Jonah's excuse was far from plausible. He admitted that he did enter the unlocked car, but only did so to take shelter from the rain. He said he had no idea he'd sat on a child while doing so. Any harm that came to the child was entirely accidental.

Bar-Jonah was given a further two years on probation, which stipulated that he had to live with his mother in Montana. He was ordered never to return to the state of Massachusetts again. A new life in Great Falls awaited Bar-Jonah, but he would continue his twisted behavior here.

However, the people of Great Falls saw Bar-Jonah as the complete opposite of who he truly was. He was a trustworthy, kind, reliable man who they allowed to babysit their children. The man was known to collect movie figurines and toys, which saw children gravitate toward him. It was only a matter of time before he struck again, but nobody could see past the jovial facade.

In the winter of 1993, he was accused of molesting a young boy he was trusted to babysit. Bar-Jonah denied the allegation and insisted if he truly were a predator, he'd have killed the child, so there were no witnesses. The police were called, but charges were ultimately dropped. Yet again, the dangerous man was free to carry out his reign of terror.

A few years later, Zachary Ramsay was walking to school on a cold February morning. It was unlike the child to truant from school, so when he didn't show up, alarm bells rang. Witnesses who saw Zachary the morning he disappeared noted that they saw a vehicle speed up as it drove in his direction, almost knocking him over. This caused the 10-year-old boy to cry before "an obese man" was seen lurking behind Zachary as he brushed himself off.

When the police were called, lead detective Bill Bellusci was immediately handed a list of registered sex offenders in the area. Bill knew better than to make his way through that list. He knew there was only one man in the area who was most likely the culprit, and who fit the witness's description: Nathaniel Bar-Jonah. Bill had been the detective on the 1993 molestation case and knew the accused was guilty. He was going to make sure the law caught up with him this time.

Remarkably, Bar-Jonah's name wasn't on the sex offenders register. His previous acts of brutality hadn't followed him to Great Falls, Montana. If he'd wanted to, he probably could've got a job in a school or nursery. These are truly troubling possibilities.

So, Bill Bellusci ordered his men to apprehend Bar-Jonah at his mother's home. They'd not obtained a warrant, so the raid proved unsuccessful. A subsequent application for a warrant was denied.

Meanwhile, the evidence that pointed to Bar-Jonah as the person responsible for Zachary's disappearance was piling up. Witnesses saw an off-white car attempt to strike the boy the day he vanished. Bar-Jonah's mother had an off-white car. The large man who'd followed Zachary around prior to his disappearance had a dark blue jacket on, akin to what a police officer would wear. Bar-Jonah was renowned for imitating law enforcement.

Not only that, but detectives found out that their prime suspect had been talking to neighbors in the days leading up to Zachary's disappearance. Bar-Jonah had dropped the young boy's name in the conversation, inquiring about him.

Bill Bellusci wasn't about to let his number one suspect slip through the net again, so he reapplied for a search warrant for Bar-Jonah's mother's. However, by this point, Bar-Jonah had figured the police were sniffing around and moved out of his mother's home. The application for the search warrant was also denied, further giving the suspect breathing room from the authorities.

With no warrant, no solid evidence to connect him to Zachary's disappearance, and no compliance from Bar-Jonah himself, the police had no choice but to allow the criminal to remain free. Naturally, he would strike again.

In the meantime, he resumed his act as the friendly neighborhood geek, showing the kids his collection of toys, figurines, and movie merchandise. It's unclear if Bar-Jonah truly had an interest in these things or if he used them as a way to lure in children. Either way, his action figures proved a big hit with the children who lived nearby, and Bar-Jonah was always more than happy to invite kids to his new home to see his collection.

In mid-December 1999, Bar-Jonah was spotted outside an elementary school. This was seen as strange since he had no children. Then, the next day, he was spotted loitering again. A few days later, he was seen hanging around the elementary school again.

The police were informed since Bar-Jonah was also dressed almost identically to a police officer. He had a gun, badge, and the recognizable blue jacket officers wore. He also had pepper spray attached to his belt. This was Bill Bellusci's time to strike. He'd waited years to capture the child molester, and he was going to seize this opportunity. He arrested Bar-Jonah for impersonating a police officer. But that wasn't enough. He needed that search warrant that he'd been denied so many times.

Again, Bill put in an application for a search warrant for Bar-Jonah's new home and his mother's. He was pessimistic that it would be approved since he'd been disappointed by the judge's decision multiple times before. However, the warrant was approved, and the police swarmed Bar-Jonah's residences.

What they'd find wouldn't surprise Bill, but it would certainly sicken him.

Bar-Jonah had a number of "police" jackets, fake badges, and other police officer gear. They found a secret area in the ceiling of the kitchen, which was accessible via a pulley. A search of the area found some disturbing evidence.

Two large photo albums, all filled with photos and cutouts of children. Among the images were also documents about BDSM.

Officers also found a separate hoard of indecent images. 3,500 of them, in fact. Bar-Jonah had also kept a list of names, all boys. Some of the boy's names matched the ones he'd already abused. Others were the names of boys who resided in Massachusetts, where Bar-Jonah had previously lived. Zackery Ramsey's name was on there. Next to it, Bar-Jonah had scrawled the word "died."

A further look into the macabre stash of evidence was an abundance of newspaper clippings about Zachary's disappearance.

The slurry of shocking evidence showed no signs of stopping.

Officers found some undeveloped film, which depicted Bar-Jonah abusing a number of boys, all of whom remain unidentified. There was also a journal with some truly horrifying entries. "Little boy stew" was one entry, and "Little boy pot pie" was another, followed by the recipe. Years prior, Bar-Jonah had confessed to his therapist that he had fantasies about dismembering and eating his victims. These entries alluded to the fact that he'd carried out those sick acts.

The final part of the search took investigators to the garage. Upon entering the space, they saw an ominous section of plywood with a distinct smell of bleach emanating from it. It was big enough to hold the body of a child. The plywood had clear indents on it, caused by a blade like a big knife or a meat cleaver. This led investigators to surmise it had been used as a chopping board for Bar-Jonah's victims.

Next, a luminol test was carried out in the garage. The test consists of using a water-based solution on the area, which then detects blood, even if it's been diluted up to 10,000 times. When the solution comes in contact with blood, it turns into a fluorescent blue.

Blood was found.

In blood, Bar-Jonah had written the name "Tita." This was thought to be in connection to the rape and murder of James Teta, a teenager whose body had been found on the Massachusetts border in 1973.

All of the evidence led to the very real notion that Bar-Jonah hadn't just been abusing and killing children — he'd been cooking and eating them, too.

A further look into Bar-Jonah's day-to-day living found some sickening proof that he wasn't the only one eating human flesh — he was feeding it to the neighborhood, too.

The man — who was, for the most part, seen as a jovial, harmless, big kid by members of the community — frequently held cookouts. He would serve burgers mostly, with neighbors commenting that they tasted "funny." When asked what meat was used, Bar-Jonah claimed they were deer burgers. He was an avid hunter, he'd say, who butchered the meat himself. It seems only half of that sentence was true.

None of the neighbors knew that Bar-Jonah hunted. Mostly because he didn't. Certainly, he'd never been seen heading out on a hunting trip, nor had he ever talked about this hobby before. The search of his property found no hunting equipment, nor did Bar-Jonah own a hunting license.

Investigators believed that the "deer meat" was, in fact, Zachary Ramsay. A look into Bar-Jonah's credit card and spending habits shows that he stopped buying food for several weeks after Zachary vanished.

The suspect also owned a meat grinder, which, upon further examination, had human hair wound up inside.

Investigators were doing the rounds, interviewing members of the community, and found that, after Zachary had disappeared, Bar-Jonah made some strange comments. "He'll never be found," he told a neighbor. "He's been chopped up and scattered." What may have sounded like a macabre observation from a tactless member of the community was, in fact, a confession.

The police also dug up the land at one of Bar-Jonah's old residences. Here, they found over 20 bones from a young boy. The identity of the boy was never uncovered.

Zachary Ramsay's mother refused to believe that Bar-Jonah had played any part in her son's disappearance. In fact, she defended the suspect. She claimed her son was still alive and was out there living his life; a psychic had convinced her the boy was in Italy. Perhaps this was the mother's way of coping. To acknowledge Bar-Jonah as the culprit would mean acknowledging her son was never coming back.

As a result, the case involving Zachary was dropped. The evidence suggesting Bar-Jonah had killed him was vast, but none of it was solid. Investigators focused on other killings the man was suspected of carrying out. They used the extensive list of boys' names found in his home, two of whom were his neighbors. Bar-Jonah had filmed his abuse of these two boys.

When the youngsters were interviewed, they admitted the man had abused them. As a result, he was charged with sexual assault and aggravated kidnapping. He was also charged with assault with a deadly weapon for using a cord to strangle one of the boys. His trial took place in 2002, which saw the monster get 130 years behind bars. He was never convicted of any murder but remains the prime suspect in a number of missing person cases.

Bar-Jonah only served six years in jail. He had a fatal heart attack, and wardens didn't find him until it was too late.

A Mile From Home

It's every parent's worst nightmare: your child making their way home from their friend's house only for their journey to be intercepted by a sadistic criminal. The child never makes it home.

Once they reach a certain age, children crave more freedom. Thinking back to your youth, you might remember the first time you rejected your parent's coddling or supervision. At some point or another, children want to be seen as "grown up."

They don't want to be driven to meet their friends or be escorted to parties. Carlie Brucia, who was in sixth grade, was beginning to get her first small taste of freedom when she would walk to and from her friend's house from the family home.

Carlie was born in March 1992 and lived with her mother and stepfather in the picturesque paradise of Sarasota, Florida. During the holidays, she would visit her biological father, who lived in New York. Her mother, Susan, doted on her.

On February 1, 2004, Carlie was hanging out with one of her friends. She'd stayed at the girl's home the night before, and the sixth graders spent the entirety of the next day together. However, it seems they'd wound up getting on one another's nerves after being in one another's company for so long and had a falling out. So, Carlie decided she'd walk home on her own.

The Brucia family only lived about a mile away. As this case shows, that's all the time a predator needs to snare their victim from the streets.

Carlie wanted to get home in time to watch the football with her family. If she had walked leisurely, the walk would have taken her about 20 minutes. The route ensured Carlie was in open spaces at all times, with passing cars and local businesses offering a shield of protection from any individuals with malignant intent for the girl.

Though, that wasn't the case.

Just after 6 p.m. that evening, she headed home. Her friend's mother called Carlie's mother to let her know her daughter was making the journey home alone. She also told Susan that the girls had a little argument, giving her a heads-up about any possible upset that occurred when she arrived home.

Susan didn't feel comfortable about her 11-year-old walking home alone. Sure, the route was fairly busy, but when it comes to most things in life, you're better off being safe rather than sorry. So, Susan sent her husband, Steven, to drive over to Bee Ridge Road and drive Carlie the rest of the way home.

Steven did a loop of the road, but there was no sign of Carlie. He did another to ensure he hadn't missed her as she walked. She was nowhere to be seen. The stepfather drove around the streets a little longer, looking for Carlie before giving up. She was gone.

However, young girls don't vanish into thin air. Susan knew something was up; Carlie wouldn't have taken off, even if she'd had a falling out with one of her friends. They were due to watch the game together as a family, with snacks and soda. Carlie wouldn't miss it.

By 7:30 p.m., Susan and Steven had searched the area entirely. They'd driven the route she would have walked and even stopped by a wooded area to scope it. They wound the vehicle's windows down and shouted Carlie's name at the top of their lungs as they trawled the area.

Susan then panickedly called the police. A search ensued, which eventually involved the help of police bloodhounds. The clever dogs led the police to Evie's Car Wash, where the search seemed to end. The police subsequently spoke to the car wash's owner and asked to review the CCTV footage from the premises in the hopes that it would offer some vital clues as to what had happened to Carlie.

Sure enough, the footage showed officers that their worst fears had been realized: the 11-year-old had been snatched in broad daylight. The footage was grainy, but it was clear enough to show Carlie being approached by a man in mechanics overalls pulling her by the arm. Frustratingly, the man had a name badge on, but the footage was too pixelated to see it clearly.

The CCTV footage was further analyzed to see if the culprit's vehicle could be traced. In the moments before Carlie's kidnapping, a yellow car was seen pulling into the car wash parking lot. Again, the footage was too grainy to verify a license plate. The cameras didn't offer a 360 view of the area, nor did they capture anything more to lead them to Carlie's abductor.

In order to track the man down, the police released the footage to the local media, and it was shown on the news. At the same time, an Amber Alert was issued.

Days passed with no leads. Susan was, as you can expect, beside herself. She had to hold on to some hope that her daughter was alive, but she knew early on that, as time passed, it was unlikely Carlie would return. All she could do was sit and wait for the police to carry out their investigation. She'd already searched the area herself and done everything she could think of to find her daughter. She had to put all her hope into the police.

Then, days after Carlie was taken, calls began rolling in after the CCTV footage had done the rounds on the local news. One name in particular kept cropping up: Joseph Smith. The 37-year-old was indeed a mechanic, and he had a lengthy rap sheet, some of which involved violent crimes toward women.

One of the people to call the police after viewing the footage was one of Joseph's colleagues. He said the man on the tape wore the same workwear as Joseph, had the same mannerisms, and bore an uncanny resemblance to him. Not only that but in the days after Carlie's vanishing, the tipster told the police that Joseph had been acting erratically. In fact, the morning after Carlie had disappeared, Joseph turned up for work under the influence of what he presumed was drugs.

The day Carlie was last seen, Joseph simply hadn't shown up for work at all.

This was the only lead officers had, so they made their way to question the suspect. Joseph was living with his friends, a married couple, Jeff and Naomi, who were letting out one of their spare rooms to him. Officers drove past the house and noticed Joseph standing outside, smoking a cigarette. The officers thought they'd do a lap around the block before pulling up to question Joseph.

When they knocked on the door, there was no answer. This was strange since they'd spotted Joseph standing outside just a minute before. He had no chance to leave, nor did he look ready to go anywhere anytime soon. The police kept knocking to no avail. After speaking with neighbors, who confirmed the man hadn't left the property, officers were convinced Joseph was inside. Surely, he could hear their knocks — they weren't being quiet when trying to get him to answer the door.

Eventually, Joseph's sister turned up. Officers approached the woman, who confirmed her brother was inside. She entered the building while officers waited outside. After a few minutes, Joseph appeared at the door, insisting he'd been asleep and didn't hear them knocking. Officers noticed that Joseph had scratches on his face and arms.

The police officers would go on to ask the suspect where he was the evening of February 1 that year. He was at home, watching football. His landlords could back him up on this, too, he said. Joseph had no idea that officers held CCTV footage showing a man looking very much like him pulling Carlie Brucia by her arm on that day. Joseph admitted the man in the footage did look like him, but he assured officers it wasn't him.

The man in the footage had a forearm full of tattoos. When officers asked Joseph to roll up his sleeves, he, too, had one arm covered in tattoos. Still, the suspect remained insistent that he'd done nothing wrong. He'd been nowhere near the car wash, he claimed.

There was another piece of intriguing evidence, though: Jeff and Naomi's yellow station wagon. As well as renting a room from the couple, it seemed Joseph also borrowed their car now and then. According to Joseph, it was a mere coincidence that the car seen at the scene of Carlie's disappearance was a yellow station wagon. When questioned if he'd used the car on February 1, Joseph admitted he had, but he hadn't gone far.

Officers needed to confirm his alibi, which they did with Naomi. This checked out. The police were sure they'd found their man but had nothing but circumstantial evidence against him. There was no solid evidence to arrest him with. Unless, of course, they found drugs on him. If they did, that would mean he'd violated his terms of probation. Sure enough, Joseph was found with drugs and syringes. He was cuffed and taken to the station.

Perhaps Joseph would crumble while in custody and admit his guilt.

Meanwhile, officers were continuing the investigation. They contacted Joseph's brother for any information, and John Smith admitted the man on the CCTV footage looked just like his brother. However, John warned the officers that if Carlie's kidnapper were indeed Joseph, they'd never get a confession out of him. It simply wasn't in him to admit his guilt.

Around the same time, the police received an interesting call from Joseph's friend and landlord, Jeff. Apparently, his wife Naomi had gotten her dates mixed up; Joseph had, in fact, borrowed their car on February 1 and didn't bring it back until the next day.

Jeff also said that he checked the odometer on the vehicle, and Joseph had done 300 miles in the car. The back seat had, unusually, been left down.

Still, there was no physical evidence tying Joseph to the crime, nor was there any sign he was going to confess. Until, on February 5, he called his brother John and contradicted his belief that he'd never confess.

Carlie's body was buried next to the Central Church of Christ, three miles from where Joseph had first taken the girl. John reiterated this confession to the police.

Investigators found her naked from the waist down, her left sock removed, with deep ligature marks on her neck. She had been violently violated prior to her murder. Carlie was removed from her vile, makeshift grave and, before being given a more humane final resting place, was autopsied.

The examiner found that the girl had been dragged to the area violently, with one side of her body filled with abrasions and cuts. They also discovered that she had been strangled from behind. Joseph Smith's semen was found on the body.

He'd also left evidence of the crime in the yellow station wagon he'd borrowed. Carlie's hair and shirt fibers were found in the vehicle. On February 20, 19 days after he'd killed the child, Joseph was indicted for first-degree murder. He also faced charges of kidnapping and capital sexual battery.

The trial took place the following November, which saw Joseph Smith receive the death by lethal injection for his vile crimes.

However, he'd never meet his maker this way. He died in July of 2021 in Raiford Prison, Florida. He was only 55, though that's still 44 more years than Carlie was ever afforded.

Law enforcement isn't convinced that Carlie was Joseph's only victim. They have also tied him to the murder of 25-year-old Tara Reilly. Her naked body was found in Bradenton, Florida, in 2000. Joseph's brother, John, is convinced his sibling carried out this crime, too. He even ruminates that, had Joseph been caught for this crime, Carlie would still be here today.

Carlie's mother found the murder of her daughter too much to bear. The death of a child will always be a world-shattering event; to live with the knowledge that they died while suffering is enough to drive a person insane. For Susan, to cope with the senseless murder of her daughter, she began using drugs. In 2007, she took a fatal dose of heroin.

Before her death, however, she worked hard to make sure Carlie's death wasn't in vain and rallied to raise awareness for abused children. However, no matter how much Susan tried to live a normal life, the pain of losing Carlie proved to be too much to bear.

Multiple Missed Opportunities

Denise Amber Goff was born in August 1986 in Englewood, Florida, to Sue and Rick Goff. Her father was an esteemed Sergeant who worked in the sheriff's office in Charlotte County, Florida. Denise was a clever, precocious little girl who grew up as a shy bookworm.

When she entered her senior year of high school, teenage Denise was asked out on a date by Nathan Lee. He was nothing at all like her. He played football, was confident, and thrived around other people. Despite Denise being quiet and being somebody who kept to herself, Nathan was able to get to know her, and the pair became inseparable.

For their first Valentine's Day as a couple, Nathan got his girlfriend a heart-shaped promise ring. She never took it off.

The high school sweethearts would go on to get engaged and have two children together. Despite their outward differences, the pair were clearly made for one another. The couple would pack their bags and take their small family to North Port, Florida, where Nathan had found work. With Denise taking care of their two young boys, Nathan had to take on three jobs to make ends meet.

Despite these struggles, the couple knew it would all be worth it in the end.

On the morning of January 17, 2008, Nathan was at work, as usual, and Denise was looking after their 2-year-old and 4-year-old. As she was cleaning the home, Nathan called her while he took his 11 am break. The couple chatted away about mundane things, including the weather. That led to Denise telling Nathan the home didn't feel well-ventilated, so she'd pushed open a few windows to let some fresh air in.

A seemingly inconsequential act that would lead to unimaginable horrors for Denise.

As was the norm, Nathan called his fiancee at 3 pm to let her know he was on his way home. Unusually, there was no answer. He pressed redial. Again, no answer. On the drive back to the family home, Nathan tried to call Denise another six times before giving up. He had a feeling in his gut that something was wrong.

He pulled up to their driveway and noticed the windows, which Denise had explicitly mentioned she was keeping open, were closed shut.

Nathan entered the home, anxious to see why his spouse wasn't answering his calls. He found her phone and house keys on a chair. Their children had been placed in the same cot, and Denise was nowhere to be seen. All kinds of scenarios were playing in Nathan's head, the most prominent one being that someone had snuck in through the open window and taken Denise. The panicked man called the police to report a possible kidnap. He then called Denise's father, Sergeant Rick Goff.

With Rick's connections, the search for Denise was expedited. Cadaver dogs were brought to the house, and a helicopter searched the local area for the 21-year-old. Officers were also tasked with knocking on neighbors' doors to see if they'd noticed anything untoward happen at the Lee household later that day.

One neighbor had noticed something strange. At roughly 2:30 pm, a green pony car had been parked in the Lee's driveway. The neighbor didn't recognize the vehicle or the man she saw getting out of it. Because it was unusual, she kept an eye on the strange car, just in case the Lees had an unwanted visitor. When she looked out of the window minutes later, the car was gone.

The woman forgot about it until she got a knock on the door from the police. Now, she had a sinking feeling she'd bore witness to her neighbor's kidnapping without realizing it.

The police searched the area all afternoon to no avail. Then, a breakthrough. At just after 6 pm that evening, a call came through to 911. It was Denise.

Denise didn't speak directly to the call handler, but she made sure the woman on the other end of the phone could hear her talking to her captor. She cleverly peppered clues and hints into the discussion she was having with the unknown man, such as the make and color of her kidnapper's car and the address she was taken from. She made it clear how she wasn't with him of her own free will and that she'd never met the man until that day.

While Denise relayed important information about herself to the operators, she was also pleading with her captor to let her go. She told him her children needed her, and she wanted to see them. Her pleas fell on deaf ears; the man had no intention of letting the woman go free.

The cell phone she'd managed to use to call 911 belonged to her captor. While Denise was on the phone, he realized his device was missing. "I don't know where your phone is, I'm sorry," Denise cried as the man demanded she find the phone.

Then, the call went dead abruptly.

Nathan and Denise's dad, Rick, asked to listen to the call to ensure the person who identified as Denise was really their Denise. Their hearts sank as they listened to the tape. Their worst fears had been realized.

Law enforcement quickly ran a tracker on the number and found the location was untraceable. The kidnapper had used a burner phone. However, many criminals are unaware that burners can still be traced back to the owner. In this case, this led the police to Michael King.

King was an unemployed divorcé from North Port, Florida. The 36-year-old was a trained plumber, but his life had taken a downward turn in the months prior to his kidnapping of Denise. He had little in the way of cash, and his home was in the process of being foreclosed.

As a child, he had an accident while sledding, which is something his family says caused his low IQ.

After kidnapping Denise, he drove her back to his home.

King used tape to tie her up before raping her. He held her in his house for hours, abusing the woman horrifically. Just under four hours later, King bundled the woman back into his car and drove to his cousin Harold's house. He asked Harold if he could borrow some items: a flashlight, a shovel, and a can of gas. Not exactly a cup of sugar, yet the cousin handed them over without question.

Then, suddenly, Denise managed to open King's car door and flung herself from the vehicle. She was, as you can imagine, hysterical. She was screaming at King's cousin to call the police, begging him to help her. She was still partially bound, and the cloth that had blindfolded her hung from her face. Harold asked King what had happened, but King nonchalantly told him it was fine and not to worry about her.

King then picked his captive up and threw her back in the car. He put the flashlight, shovel, and gas in the trunk and sped off. Harold didn't intervene, but he did tell his daughter, who was in the house, what he'd seen. The 17-year-old had the gumption to convince her father to call the police. Harold relented, though he chose to use a payphone to remain anonymous, and gave them Michael King's details, describing the kidnapping he had just witnessed.

As a result, officers attended King's property. The unkempt house had one room in particular that was of interest. Officers found large segments of tape with a woman's hair stuck to it, rolled up into a ball.

Meanwhile, King was speeding through the streets with his captive in the car, and his erratic behavior caught the attention of fellow driver Jane Kowalski. As King pulled up beside Jane at the traffic lights, she looked over to his vehicle and noticed his right hand aggressively pushing something down in the backseat. Whoever he was restraining was fighting hard against the man, though she proved no match for his strength. Jane was worried she'd witnessed a child being taken, especially when she heard high-pitched screams.

Jane called the police. This was now the fourth call to law enforcement, with each call offering strong clues to lead the police to the culprit. One of the calls had been from Denise herself, the other was from someone who named the suspect, and now Jane was calling and offering the police the make and model of a car that she witnessed a kidnapping in.

King noticed Jane was on the phone while the pair were parked up alongside one another. The woman didn't hide the fact she was looking at him. She did her best to get a clear view of his number plate. However, King was on to her and slowed down enough to ensure Jane had to drive ahead of him before he took an abrupt left turn. The concerned woman was unable to find the vehicle again.

Then, radio silence for three hours.

Just after 9 pm that night, however, King was finally pulled over by the police. The officer on duty shone his flashlight into the back of the car and saw a shovel. It had recently been used. When the officer shone his light up and down King, it was clear he was soaking wet from the waist down, and his footwear had clumps of mud falling from them. It was a sinister scene, ominous enough for the officer to place King in cuffs.

Then, after searching the suspect, the officer found the burner phone. The battery had been taken out of it, as had the SIM card. King was brought to the station and questioned over Denise's disappearance.

The man would offer a strange story. He said that he and Denise had both been kidnapped together by an unknown man. In fact, King said, it was he who had snuck his phone to Denise and allowed her to call 911.

King's cousin, Harold, came to the police station and tried to get him to tell the truth. Again, King reiterated he was the victim, not the criminal. Harold suggested that King take a lie detector test, which the suspect declined to do.

It was clear that King was lying. There was still some, albeit tiny, hope that Denise would be found alive. But things weren't looking good.

For the next two days, law enforcement trawled the area where King had been arrested. In particular, they focused on a muddy, desolate area nearby, using cadaver dogs to help them find the woman. On January 19, the Lee and Goff families got the news they'd been dreading: Denise's body had been found.

She was naked in a swampy, shallow grave. King had only driven 5 miles from the area where Jane Kowalski had spotted him. Denise's death had been caused by a single bullet to the head.

King's picture was on the front page of The Daily Sun the following day. When retrieving her morning paper, Jane Kowalski got a shock; staring back at her was the same man she'd seen days prior, smothering somebody in the back seat of his car. She immediately called 911 and told them this was the man she'd called them about a few days ago.

However, the 911 operator had no idea what she was talking about.

In a catalog of tragic events, it seems Jane's original 911 call wasn't reported back. When the North Port Police Department investigated why nobody was dispatched to the location Jane had offered them, it seemed a "chaotic environment" and "shift changes" were to blame. The dispatchers involved were suspended, though they weren't fired. Sheriff John Davenport would refer to the blunder as a "missed opportunity."

The tale gets even more frustrating. At the time of Jane's 911 call, a patrol car was on the exact street King had driven down to evade Jane's following him. If the call had been dispatched correctly, that patrol car would have apprehended King. Denise would likely have been saved, and her two boys would have their mother with them today.

Despite King's waffling story about him and Denise — two people who'd never crossed paths before — being kidnapped by an unknown assailant, there was no escaping the pile of evidence presented to him. He was charged with kidnapping, sexual battery, and first-degree murder, all of which he pleaded not guilty to.

His defense team argued that the sledding incident from his childhood had rendered him brain-damaged, and his IQ was 71, which is classed as borderline intellectual functioning. I always find it odd when prosecutors use low IQ as a defense.

I fail to understand the rationale. Throughout my life, I've met people with lower IQs and dealt with people with below-average IQs. All of them have had consciences, understood right from wrong, and were able to understand the consequences of doing something irreversible. Low IQ does not equate to delinquency. Low IQ can make it hard for individuals to problem-solve and plan ahead. They often have a poor memory. Their vocabulary is perhaps limited. In my opinion, it does not alleviate any guilt of a serious crime they may commit.

Both cousin Harold and key witness Jane Kowalski testified against King at the trial. Even if they hadn't, the evidence against him was enough to seal his fate. His DNA was found on Denise's body.

The autopsy results were hard to hear for Denise's family. She had been raped in a horrific manner prior to being driven to her death. She had numerous defense wounds on her body. Her wrists and feet were bruised and bloody from the tape that bound her.

Her death, despite being from a bullet to the head, wasn't quick. Despite the single bullet causing one of her eyes to explode, the woman was alive for a while after the shot. Her lungs had accumulated blood, meaning she'd laid breathing after King had shot her point blank.

In the back of King's car was Denise's heart-shaped promise ring. It was tightly lodged between the seats. She'd never, ever taken it off before. It seems, in order to ensure her murderer was caught, she'd planted it as evidence.

In December 2009, King was found guilty of the kidnapping, rape, and murder of Denise Amber Lee. He was handed the death penalty. He remains on death row.

In a bid to ensure the blunders and mistakes that allowed King to carry out Denise's killing weren't repeated, Nathan Lee began the Denise Amber Lee Foundation. The foundation rallied for better 911 call center training. The Denise Amber Lee Act was introduced, which sees call handlers receive over 200 hours of operator training.

In 2012, Nathan received $1.25 million from the Charlotte County 911 department for mishandling the calls. He has since found love again and resides with his wife and children in Englewood, Florida.

The Beauty Queen Killer

A race car driver with hordes of money, properties, and expensive vehicles isn't what you immediately think of when it comes to the typical serial killer profile. If anything, killer Christopher Wilder turns the stereotypical serial killer description on its head. He was successful, dated supermodels, and had a career he'd dreamed of since his youth.

Still, he was a serial rapist, a murderer, and harbored a deep resentment for women. Wilder got away with his crimes for years, playing the role of a charming bachelor while simultaneously ruining the lives of women who were unfortunate enough to cross his path.

Wilder was born in March 1945 in Sydney, Australia. He was born with dual citizenship since his father was a naval officer from the US, and his mother was an Australian national. Little is known about Wilder's upbringing, so this horrific tale begins when he was 17. He'd just been arrested for his participation in a gang rape.

In January 1963, Wilder was apprehended for his assault on the 13-year-old, which didn't see him receive any jail time. Instead, he received probation. As you may recall from the Bar-Jonah chapter, it seems when an individual with perverted desires is given the proverbial slap on the wrist upon being caught for the first time; it only bolsters their ability to continue with it. This is certainly the case for Wilder.

While on probation, it's alleged that Wilder received electroshock therapy to treat his sexual disorder. If true, it seems the therapy did nothing to quell his tendencies. If anything, it just gave him torturous inspiration for one of his future victims. However, the claims of undergoing electroshock treatment came directly from Wilder himself, and honesty wasn't at the forefront of his mind when relaying stories.

In fact, it's even alleged he lied about pointless things from childhood, such as a near-drowning incident he was involved in. There is no proof this ever happened.

After his brush with the law, it seems Wilder laid low for a while. At the very least, he wasn't caught for any sexual crimes he may have committed during this time, but the more you learn about Wilder, the more you may assume there must have been some unreported crimes he carried out during this period.

At the age of 23, in 1968, Wilder met a woman he'd go on to marry. She left him after a week. After all, during their short marriage, he sexually assaulted her, beat her, and allegedly even tried to end her life. His former spouse, though perhaps she didn't realize at the time, had a very lucky escape. Her fate could have been much, much worse had she stayed with him.

Wilder was an intelligent man with an entrepreneurial spirit. He liked the finer things in life and decided he wanted to have them. So, the following year, in 1968, he moved to Boynton Beach, Florida, to realize his dream of living a hedonistic life. It seems Wilder adopted a "fake it until you make it" attitude since Boynton Beach has one of Florida's most affluent zip codes. The area is filled with upscale, palm tree-lined homes sitting close to some of the state's most popular beaches. At this point in time, Wilder was yet to make it.

However, he did make it—a lot of money, in fact. He found his fortune in construction work and then real estate, which afforded him the luxuries he'd desired his whole life. He bought a speedboat and a sports car and kitted out his bachelor pad with the latest furnishings.

It's a true crime trope, often reserved for victims, but Christopher Wilder truly had the world at his feet.

But it wasn't enough.

One of Wilder's hobbies was amateur photography. Namely, he liked to photograph women. He would trawl the beaches, ogling the sun-kissed, bikini-clad women, and offer them a photoshoot. As you can imagine, he faced plenty of rejections, though, in 1974, one young woman took him up on his offer.

She went back to his home with him, and from the outside, it looked legit. It was big, filled with expensive toys and furniture, and gave the girl confidence that Wilder really was a professional photographer. Perhaps this would be her big break.

Instead, it was a nightmarish hell for the young woman. Wilder had spiked her drink. Once the woman had succumbed to the cocktail, he violated her. He set her free once he was done with his depravity.

Again, he got away with the crime. It seemed the man began feeling invincible. He was getting away with crime after crime, and even when the police were involved, there was little in the way of consequences. So, his actions would only become more depraved.

Wilder's crimes spanned countries, with him going on to offend in his home city of Sydney, Australia. He returned home to see his parents in 1982 and was captured by the police after luring two teenagers from Manly Beach and forcing them to pose naked for his "photo shoot." His parents posted his bail, and Wilder fled back to Florida. His court date for the crime was postponed several times, and he would never end up taking the stand for this offense.

It seemed Wilder was immune to the law. He had the funds to simply jet off if he found himself in trouble and even when he did, his parents bailed him out. Plus, as he was discovering, few of his victims went to the police after their ordeals with him.

In 1983, after his return to Florida, two young girls, aged 10 and 12, would go to the police about a man who'd forced them to perform sex acts on him. After being shown several mugshots of known sex offenders in the area, both girls pinpointed Wilder as their attacker.

Still, the serial sex offender managed to evade the police. Perhaps he knew his days free were numbered, or perhaps he didn't believe the police would ever lock him up; either way Wilder decided to embark on a criminal cross-country trip. This road trip would see him kidnap, rape, and murder women at a rapid pace.

The sick spree began on February 26, 1984, when Wilder was attending the Miami Grand Prix. Here, 20-year-old Rosario Gonzales was working as a spokesmodel. She was last seen leaving the race with a man fitting Wilder's description. Her car was found parked not far away from the track, and Rosario was sadly never found.

Just over a week later, one of Wilder's former girlfriends disappeared. Her name was Elizabeth Kenyon, a former Miss Florida finalist, and she'd previously rejected Wilder's offer of marriage. It seems this rejection was something the vengeful man was unable to swallow. He met up with her on March 5 and was seen talking to his ex at a gas station. The gas station attendant suggested Elizabeth and Wilder's interaction looked normal and even friendly.

It appears Wilder had snared his victim under the cloak of familiarity. She would never be seen again.

Elizabeth's family called the police to report the woman missing. However, law enforcement had little in the way of evidence that would lead them to her. Plus, Elizabeth was 23 years old. The police reasoned with the Kenyon family that young women leave their home city all the time. Perhaps Elizabeth had left for pastures new. However, the Kenyon family knew she wouldn't do this. So, they hired a private investigator to find out what had really happened to her.

The trail led the investigator directly to Christopher Wilder. Instead of confronting the suspect face to face, as he was incredibly elusive, the PI called him and began asking questions about Elizabeth Kenyon.

This was enough to unnerve Wilder, who quickly made his way out of Boynton Beach to the coastal city of Indian Harbour, two hours away from his home. It was a trick that had worked before; moving away from a location seemingly abolished the criminal of facing any comeuppance.

Two weeks after Elizabeth Kenyon was last seen, yet another girl vanished. 21-year-old Theresa "Terry" Ferguson vanished from Merritt Island. She was last seen at a mall with a man who looked just like Christopher Wilder.

Unlike the other victims, her body would be found just days later. She was floating in a canal in Canaveral Groves, her face so violently beaten that she was unrecognizable. In fact, her dental records had to be used to formally identify her.

The sick killer was quite literally getting away with murder. Despite plenty of witnesses who were able to pinpoint Wilder as the man last seen with the missing young women, no arrest was made. Wilder was too wily for the police, flitting from location to location without any trouble from law enforcement.

His next attack would occur on March 20. Student Linda Grover was forced into Wilder's car after she turned down his offer to take professional photos of her. Linda declined as politely as she could, but that made no difference to Wilder's response. He beat the young woman until she was subdued enough to bundle in the car. He bound her by the hands and encased her in a blanket before driving her to Glen Oaks in Sarasota.

He forced her into a dank motel room where he raped her. He also tortured the terrified young woman. He super glued her eyes shut, sealing the adhesive with a hairdryer. He also strapped some copper wires to her feet and electrocuted her. Despite the difference in physical power, Linda fought back as hard as she could. The pain and terror she must've felt didn't squash the woman's will to fight. The more she fought, the more Wilder beat her.

However, at one point during a beating, she was able to lock herself in the bathroom. While blinded and beaten, she screamed as loud as she could. She banged on the bathroom walls with all the strength she could muster. Panicked at Linda bringing attention to the torture room and unable to get into the bathroom, Wilder raced to his car and fled.

One of the main things you're taught when approached by a stranger who's trying to lure you somewhere is to scream and make as much noise as possible. This way, the would-be attacker is spooked at the prospect of having witnesses or being apprehended, so they abandon their sinister plans.

In this instance, Linda has already endured a horrific ordeal at Wilder's hands, but the same principle applies. She brought as much attention as she possibly could to her location, ultimately saving herself.

The badly beaten woman was rescued, and she was able to pick a picture of Wilder out of a stack of mugshots she was given by the police.

Wilder knew he had to get out of the state. He drove 14 hours from Sarasota to Beaumont, Texas. Would he lay low here? No.

Almost as soon as he arrived, he was back on the prowl. Terry Walden was a 23-year-old nursing student who had the misfortune of being approached by Wilder to use her as a model in one of his upcoming photoshoots. By some miracle, she managed to escape this interaction with her life. The young mother had no interest in posing for a random, scantily clad photoshoot, much less with someone she didn't know behind the camera.

When the young woman got home to her husband, she mentioned the bizarre interaction she'd had with a big-bearded Australian who'd tried soliciting her for nude photos.

However, Wilder, as we now know, doesn't take rejection well.

He found the young woman again a few days later and plucked her from the street. She was found on March 26 in a canal. She'd been raped before being stabbed to death. To add insult to injury, Wilder was now driving about in Terry's vehicle. It's almost like he was goading the police, believing he had a cloak of immunity surrounding him.

Using his latest victim's rust-colored car, Wilder took himself to Oklahoma City, where he abducted 21-year-old Suzanne Logan. Again, he locked her in the trunk of the car, booked a room at a cheap inn, and violated the young woman. Suzanne was trapped with the sadistic man for almost 24 hours before he drove her to a reservoir and stabbed her to death.

Wilder had dumped Terry's car by now, and the police had found it abandoned. A subsequent forensic analysis of it found some of the previous victim, Theresa Ferguson's DNA inside. This tied her murder directly to Wilder. Still, the police were no closer to catching the serial predator.

Mere days later, 18-year-old Sheryl Bonaventura would fall prey to Wilder, who had now made it to Colorado. She was seen with Wilder at a diner and then checking in together at a motel. It seems the teenager believed the 39-year-old's spiel about being a famous photographer and went with him to take some pictures. She was found raped, shot and stabbed.

In between driving from state to state and violating any young woman who crossed his path, Christopher Wilder found time to attend a fashion show in Las Vegas on April 1. The trip, naturally, wasn't to admire the fashion or gain inspiration for his "portfolio." It was to obtain another victim. Wilder was successful and snared Michelle Korfman, a teenager who dreamed of being a model.

She was found the following month. Her death had been unlike the others; she'd been suffocated to death with soil, which clogged her larynx and trachea. She was killed in California's Angeles National Forest, and the blazing sun she was exposed to meant her body had decomposed rapidly in just a month. She had to be identified by dental records.

By April 3, Wilder was on the FBI's Ten Most Wanted list. Young girls were being tortured, abused, and slain by the sadist in quick succession, and the police were always a step behind him. This didn't faze Wilder. Two days after killing Michelle, he abducted Tina Risico, a 16-year-old from Torrance, California. This time, though, Wilder changed tack.

He abused the girl, but he didn't kill her. He saw her as an opportunity to acquire new victims. He promised to keep her alive as long as she lured more young girls for him to abuse. Faced with doing this or being slaughtered, Tina did what she had to in order to survive. Wilder drove his latest victim to Indiana, where she aided him in abducting 16-year-old Dawnette Wilt. For over 48 hours, Dawnette was subjected to heinous abuse and sadism at Wilder's hands.

Tina drove her captor and the other victim around until Wilder decided it was time to get rid of Dawnette. He took her to a remote woods in New York and stabbed her. He threw her lifeless body to the floor before leaving the scene.

Only, she hadn't died.

Dawnette wrapped her jeans around her wounds and somehow made it to the roadside. Thankfully, a passerby spotted her and took the teenager to hospital. She needed emergency surgery, but she made it through her ordeal.

Meanwhile, Wilder was having doubts as to whether Dawnette had actually died. Something had convinced him he'd left her clinging to life, so he returned to the scene of the murder to discover it was, in fact, the scene of an attempted murder. The spot he'd left her in was empty. She'd managed to survive the attack. Wilder knew it was time to flee.

Hours later, Dawnette was coming around from life-saving surgery and was able to tell the police everything she knew. One key piece of information she had was that Wilder was planning to cross the border into Canada.

Before he did, Wilder was going to snare one more victim. Beth Dodge, a 33-year-old from New York, would fall foul to Wilder's depraved desires. She was found shot in a gravel pit.

Wilder decided it was time to get rid of Tina. As promised, he'd refrained from killing her and bought her a ticket to LAX. They parted ways at Boston Airport. Wilder then made his way to New Hampshire. He stopped off at a gas station in Colebrook, where he was recognized by state troopers. By this point, Wilders mugshot was all over the news and plastered around shops and malls. The two men approached Wilder, though he noticed them, and jumped into his car, ready to flee yet again.

However, one of the state troopers managed to grab hold of Wilder, preventing him from driving off. By this point, Wilder had already managed to grab his handgun and fired two shots. One of them went through the state trooper. Both went through Wilder, killing him almost instantly.

The state trooper was injured, though not fatally.

Nobody knows if he killed himself on purpose to avoid a lifetime behind bars or if he did it accidentally in the scuffle. However, it did mean that none of Wilders' many, many victims would be able to confront him on the stand, nor would any of his deceased victims see any form of judicial justice.

Wilder killed eight women that we know of. It's assumed he's killed many more than that figure. He's the prime suspect in a number of other crimes, such as the 1965 Wanda Beach murders. This would certainly fit with Wilder's MO.

The beach, in New South Wales, Australia, was the brutal crime scene of the murder of two teenage girls. Wilder is also thought to be responsible for the murder of 15-year-old Colleen Osborn, who was found dead in Florida in 1984.

There are over a dozen unsolved murder cases that police believe were committed by Christopher Wilder. However, Wilder took all knowledge of his crimes to his grave with him.

By shooting himself, intentionally or not, Wilder took a predator off the streets. There may not be a more fitting event for the phrase, "The trash took itself out."

The Bus Ride From Hell

In the summer of 2008, Timothy McLean boarded a Greyhound bus from Edmonton to his hometown of Winnipeg. The Canadian was tired and looking forward to getting home. He'd been working at the carnival in Edmonton, and his stint was finally over. The late-night bus was sparse with travelers, but another man got aboard the vehicle at some point during Tim's journey: 40-year-old Vincent Li.

Unbeknownst to Tim, Li was a schizophrenic who was suffering severe delusions. Li would carry out an unprovoked nightmarish attack on Tim, which saw the young man killed and cannibalized while stuck on the moving bus.

As Tim boarded the bus that fateful night, he found his way to the back so he could relax on the lengthy journey home. He picked a seat close to the toilets, flung his bag on the seat, and collapsed next to it. Tim planned on crashing out for most of the journey. He'd had a long few months and was ready to have some respite in Winnipeg.

He got comfortable and pulled his headphones on. He rested his head and zoned out. As Tim wound down across the two seats he'd sprawled himself across, he thought about being reunited with his girlfriend. She was pregnant with their first child, a boy.

He paid little attention to the passengers who got on and off the bus. He flitted from sleep to looking out the window, with buses rarely being comfortable enough to get 40 winks on.

When Vince Li got on the bus in Erickson, Manitoba, again, Tim paid little heed to the new person on the bus. Li sat at the front while Tim was still at the back, trying to ensure he was well-rested before being reunited with his family. Other passengers noticed something strange about Li's demeanor, however. He seemed to be agitated and bewildered. He moved about the bus and eventually settled next to Tim.

There were any number of free seats on the bus, but he chose to park himself next to a sleeping man. Tim still had his headphones on and was using the window as a pillow. At first, he was unaware that Li was sitting next to him.

The pair sat together for a while before Li pulled a large knife he'd been concealing and frantically began stabbing Tim in the chest and neck. The other passengers heard the commotion and looked to the back; what they saw was utterly disturbing. Li was in a frenzy, and Tim was covered in blood.

The bus driver quickly pulled over, and all but one of the passengers — aside from the attacker and victim — fled the bus. One young man tried in vain to get Li off a limp Tim. However, Li had a knife that he was waving and slashing indiscriminately, and it was clear he was ready to strike again if anyone tried to stop him.

With everyone now off the bus, it was just Tim and Li aboard. Nobody could get back on the bus, but then Li couldn't get off the bus either. Though, it didn't seem as if he minded. He would pace up and down the aisle, intimidating the crowd of passengers congregating outside the bus.

Then, Li returned to Tim and began sawing his neck. He completely decapitated him. After severing Tim's head, Li held it up for the sickened bystanders to witness. He then resumed hacking away at Tim, cutting off several sections of his flesh before consuming it. The passengers were equal parts sickened by what they were seeing and frustrated there was nothing they could do to stop it.

Some of them found themselves vomiting at the roadside after witnessing the gory attack and horrific displays of cannibalism.

The Royal Canadian Mounted Police eventually arrived at the scene, and by this point, it was clear Li wanted to escape the scene of the crime. However, the bus driver and another passenger had enlisted the help of a passing truck driver, who'd given them a crowbar and some tools to use as defense weapons. If Li tried to disembark, he knew he was outnumbered.

So, Li tried to drive off with the bus. The quick-thinking driver had already engaged the emergency immobilizer system, meaning Li was going nowhere fast. One can only dread to think of the number of additional casualties that would've occurred had the driver not demobilized the vehicle. It seems Li realized he was trapped on the bus, as he was overheard saying to himself, "I have to stay on the bus forever."

Li's desire to further mutilate the corpse showed no signs of waning. He would alternate from pacing the aisle of the bus to attacking Tim's body.

Eventually, after a five-hour standoff, Li decided to make a break for it. He smashed one of the windows in an attempt to flee, but as he did, he was shot by the Royal Canadian Mounted Police with a taser. The killer was dragged from the smashed window and cuffed. A pat down of the man revealed he had Tim's nose, tongue, and one of his ears in his pockets. He was quickly detained in the back of a police car and taken in for questioning.

Police embarked on the bus and found Tim's horrifically mutilated body. Some of his body parts were strewn in plastic bags by Li. Tim's eyes were missing, as was a section from his heart. Li was asked if he'd consumed these body parts also, but he heatedly denied doing so. However, there is no other explanation for their disappearance since they weren't found on the bus or in Li's person. We can only presume that Li did, in fact, eat them.

Disturbed passengers were interviewed before being taken to their destination of Winnipeg. Witnesses noted that Li wasn't full of anger when he attacked Tim. He was calm and collected, and he treated killing his victim like any other transaction. One witness described Li as being like a "robot."

Canada was rocked by the crime. It was unlike any other that had occurred before, and naturally, they wanted to know why such an attack happened. *Did Li know Tim? Had there been some kind of altercation? Was Li on drugs?*

Li would tell the police that God himself had told him to carry out the attack. According to Li, an alien invasion was about to take place, and he was the chosen one to protect humans from the pending attack. The voice also told Li to prepare for the war by traveling, which he did. He would leave his wife for days on end as he embarked on journeys across the country. His wife would corroborate what Li was saying. She confirmed that her husband made little sense when he spoke in the lead-up to the attack. He'd ramble and make wild claims about an alien invasion.

As a result of these fears, his wife said, he began traveling with a knife for protection.

While on one of his many adventures across Canada, Li spotted Tim on the bus, and the voice again barked an order at him: destroy the alien. According to Li, he believed Tim was both a demon and an extraterrestrial and needed to be destroyed, as per the orders from the voice. When asked why he felt the need to mutilate Tim's body, Li claimed it was to prevent him from regenerating.

There was no denying that Li was responsible for killing Tim, but by law, he was unable to be tried for murder since he was mentally ill.

In March 2009, almost a year after the murder, Li was committed to the Selkirk Mental Health Centre.

Tim's family was upset with the ruling. Their son had been killed in a barbaric way, and his corpse was mutilated beyond recognition, yet they felt his killer had completely evaded justice. "There was nobody else on that bus holding a knife, slicing up my child," Tim's mother Carol would say.

Still, there was one big reason for Carol to keep it together—her grandson, whom Tim never had the chance to meet. When she looks at her grandson, she sees Tim, and this gives her comfort. She now has full custody of her grandson, whom she believes was a gift from Tim.

Tim's dad would honor his son's memory by getting a tattoo of his face across his heart.

In 2014, Corporal Ken Barker, who served with The Royal Canadian Mounted Police, killed himself. He was one of the officers called to the scene of Tim's murder. His family stated that he'd suffered PTSD from the horrors he'd witnessed that day.

In 2017, less than ten years after the murder took place, Vincent Li was discharged from the Selkirk facility. His release is unconditional; he's no longer seen as a danger to anyone. He doesn't have to have any counseling, monitoring, or attend any kind of regular review. His release was controversial, and Tim's mother was vocal about her disapproval of the decision. There was even a public petition to keep him in the facility.

Li has since changed his name and lives alone in the Canadian province of Manitoba.

Final Thoughts

Thank you for reading *Unbelievable Crimes Volume Ten*.

Many of these cases have been difficult to research, particularly since many of them contain the grotesque element of sexual abuse. Only when the book comes together, do I realize how many chapters contain similar themes. In this instance, the macabre theme is sexual assault.

Murder is awful enough, but to know the victim endured perverse hell prior to their demise makes these cases even more upsetting. When it involves a child, such as in the case of Carlie Brucia, the feelings of disgust toward the perpetrator are even greater.

Though these crimes are difficult to digest, I strongly feel as though they should be retold as the years go by. To forget them is to forget the victim's suffering. When we forget how such tragedies occur, they are doomed to be repeated.

Once again, I'd like to thank you for reading and let you know how much I value your continued readership. If you find the time to leave a review, that would be so helpful for me and I'd be extremely grateful.

I hope you enjoyed this tenth installment of the series. If so, book eleven will be released shortly.

I've taken some time to reflect on the series as a whole and consider its future direction after this volume.

I've realized that longer publications would likely better serve the series. I initially believed that nine, ten, or 11 stories per publication was enough to keep you, the reader, interested and reading until the end. Any more, and I feared you may get bored or, worse, leave an unfinished book.

Or, so I thought, anyway.

However, moving forward for this series, I'll be covering 20 cases per book. From Volume Eleven onward, Unbelievable Crimes will have around double the number of cases compared to previous installments. I have enough—a whole spreadsheet, in fact—material for at least the next half a dozen books.

Volume Eleven includes some truly shocking stories, a few of which were new to me before I researched them. I hope to see you there!

Once again, thank you for your readership, fellow true crime follower!

Until next time,

Daniela

My newsletter sign-up link:

Danielaairlie.carrd.co[1]

---

1. http://danielaairlie.carrd.co

Don't miss out!

Visit the website below and you can sign up to receive emails whenever Daniela Airlie publishes a new book. There's no charge and no obligation.

https://books2read.com/r/B-A-GFMW-UVJAD

BOOKS 2 READ

Connecting independent readers to independent writers.

Also by Daniela Airlie

Infamous Crimes
Infamous Cults: The Life and Crimes of Cult Leaders and Their Followers

Unbelievable Crimes
Unbelievable Crimes Volume One: Macabre Yet Unknown True Crime Stories
Unbelievable Crimes Volume Two: Macabre Yet Unknown True Crime Stories
Unbelievable Crimes Volume Three: Macabre Yet Unknown True Crime Stories
Unbelievable Crimes Volume Four: Macabre Yet Unknown True Crime Stories
Unbelievable Crimes Volume Five: Macabre Yet Unknown True Crime Stories
Unbelievable Crimes Volume Six: Macabre Yet Unknown True Crime Stories
Unbelievable Crimes Volume Seven
Unbelievable Crimes Volume Eight

Unbelievable Crimes Volume Nine
Unbelievable Crimes Volume Ten

www.ingramcontent.com/pod-product-compliance
Lightning Source LLC
Chambersburg PA
CBHW072100110526
44590CB00018B/3258